Paupers' New York

Miles Turner was born and brought up in Manhattan, and returns when nostalgia gets the better of him. He has definite ideas about what is best and worst about the city, and the energy and enthusiasm to write them down. His earlier book, *Paupers' Paris*, is also available in Pan.

Miles Turner

Paupers'
New York

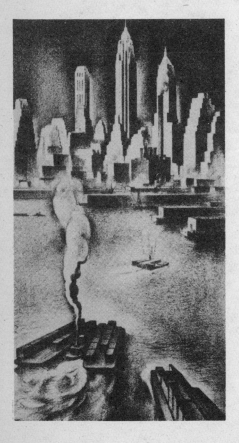

Pan Original
Pan Books London and Sydney

First published 1986 by Pan Books Ltd
Cavaye Place, London SW10 9PG
9 8 7 6 5 4 3 2 1
© Miles Turner 1986
ISBN 0 330 29140 8
Printed and bound in Great Britain by
Cox & Wyman Ltd, Reading

Contents

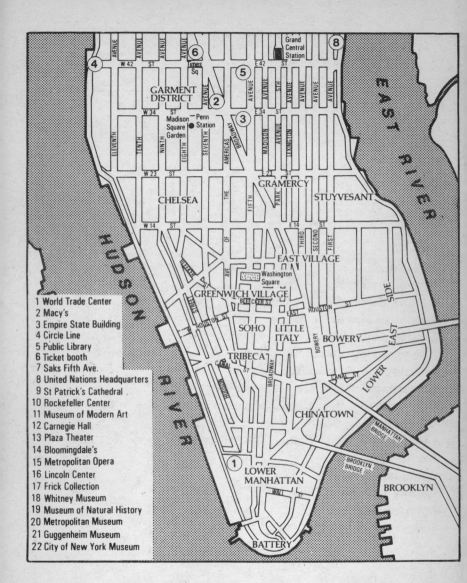

1 World Trade Center
2 Macy's
3 Empire State Building
4 Circle Line
5 Public Library
6 Ticket booth
7 Saks Fifth Ave.
8 United Nations Headquarters
9 St Patrick's Cathedral
10 Rockefeller Center
11 Museum of Modern Art
12 Carnegie Hall
13 Plaza Theater
14 Bloomingdale's
15 Metropolitan Opera
16 Lincoln Center
17 Frick Collection
18 Whitney Museum
19 Museum of Natural History
20 Metropolitan Museum
21 Guggenheim Museum
22 City of New York Museum

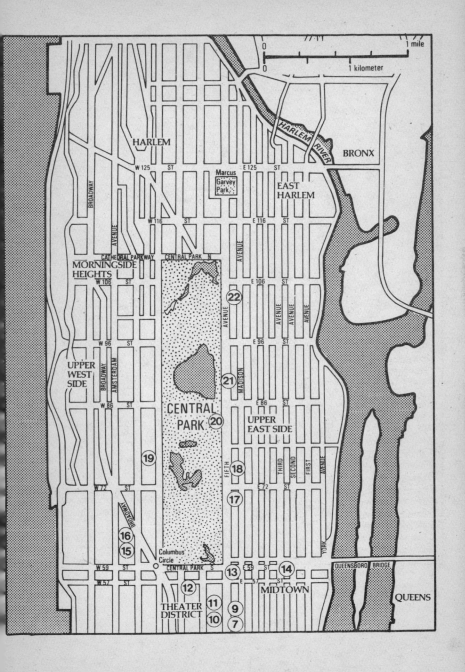

Introduction

It probably hasn't escaped your notice that the east side of the Atlantic is sinking under the weight of American tourists, all of them riding an exaggeratedly strong dollar, snapping up Napoleon's Tomb and the Albert Memorial and shipping them back to Scarsdale, brick by brick. It's like the Russian pogroms and the Irish potato famines in reverse, without the vexations of steerage. This is the year that everyone has decided to escape from New York – which means it's an excellent time for you to escape *to* New York.

The neatness of this solution does have a minor flaw: New York is so ridiculously expensive that no one, no matter how rich, can afford to live there. If you're living on the brink of pauperhood in your own country, how can you possibly avoid being consigned to the lower depths in Manhattan? Answer: The same way everyone else in New York does – by mobilizing a weather eye for discounts and bargains, massive doses of low cunning, and an inborn ability to appreciate the glories of the city without actually paying for them.

If you can pull this off, you'll have no trouble sidestepping the city's bear-traps and finding your way into its more interesting exhibits, not the least of which is its street-life. For mad, precipitous rushes of adrenalin, nothing else even comes close to New York. It's where everything begins in America, and where everything ultimately hatches: commerce, industry, fashion, art, music, theatre, dance, the works. It's elegant, blasé, hard-edged, avant-garde, sophisticated, smart, and tingling with nervous energy. It's also noisy, dirty, rough, rude, exuberant and alive – the last frontier, the greatest show on earth.

You'll discover that New York is anything but a tourist town, even though at any given moment it has probably more newcomers than long-term residents . . . It's more a place in which to seek your fortune than to see the sights; and though the sights are awesome, they're strictly incidental. To avoid being pushed around – or treated like a tourist – it's a good idea at least to look as if you have important business to conduct, crucial meetings to attend – a mission in life, even if it's only window-shopping at Lord & Taylor or calling on the lions in the Bronx Zoo. True natives are few on the ground, so you don't have to feel at a disadvantage if you weren't actually born in Hell's Kitchen or Gramercy Square. Hardly anyone else was, either: it's a city of latecomers. There's no need to renounce your present circumstances and move to New York, but it doesn't hurt to spend your time in the city as if you had.

The way to enjoy life in New York is to get into the act: keep pace with the traffic, keep your wits about you, screen out the incivilities and stay tuned to the human comedy. Develop an ear for the quintessential dialogue of the streets and an eye for the infinite variety of New York characters and types. There was never such a paradise for eavesdroppers. Above all, don't be afraid to make contact. New Yorkers are maligned and misunderstood – hence a bit flinty on the surface – and they're inevitably surprised and flattered when strangers ask directions or advice. Once the approach has been made, most will go overboard to make you feel at home in the city – even to the extent of arguing with other passers-by on how best to help you, or steering you wrong out of simple kindness and sheer inability to confess ignorance of any subject.

You'll notice that 'the city' is a term that all New Yorkers use for the island-borough of Manhattan, the pure distillation of New York. Except for a few brief forays into the other boroughs, this book won't take you much farther afield – and a 'comprehensive' view of New York is out of the question. The city has about a six-month metamorphic cycle: the very buildings you once considered landmarks are liquidated and replaced before you have time to miss them. Shops and restaurants spring up with the morning dew and are boarded over by nightfall. Prices, stock items, menus, staff and management of every commercial venture – to say nothing of trends and fashions – fluctuate with the merest caprice – so don't be surprised if what you read here today is gone – or too mobbed to get through the doors – by tomorrow.

This book owes everything to the collaboration and forbearance of all my friends and relations: especially to Ann and Don Fletcher and Polly Rowles, who put me up (and put up with me) in the city; to my mother, Martha Lomask, for scouting out routes, packages and prices in London; to Charlie White, for turning a blind eye (again) to my sudden and prolonged absences from his office; to Robert Mercer, for ingenious solutions to insoluble problems and candid reading of every draft; to Dorothy Arrigo, Darcy Elman, Ann and Don Fletcher, Paul Handelman, Madalynne Reuter, Polly Rowles, Paul Urban, Dawn White, Joyce Wilson and Leonard Yoon for ideas and inspirations; and to Hetty Thistlewaite and Annie Jackson, for deft editing and unlimited patience.

Preliminaries

Who

New York is packed with humanity, but if you're not naturally gregarious it can be the world's loneliest city. New Yorkers are not unfriendly, they're just in a hurry. Apartment-dwellers don't seem to know their neighbours; transactions in shops can be made wordlessly, even without eye contact; and New York crowds have an isolating effect. As a general rule, you'll find it all too easy to be left alone in New York – it's finding company that takes ingenuity and effort. Before you arrive, you should decide whether you want to import your own company – friends, relatives, compatriots – or take pot luck in the city. Some advantages and disadvantages:

Travelling alone allows you to move about at your own pace, on your own schedule, and in your own direction. Once you know your way around, there is a genuine rush of pride in being able to navigate the city on your own, but no one else to blame for bad judgments, and no one else to share the glory of your triumphs. Crossing Central Park alone at dusk, for example, is about even with the charge of the Light Brigade for sheer guts and temerity. It provides the kind of *frisson* available only to the loner in New York. If this is your meat, by all means travel alone.

Travelling in company allows you to compare notes and share pleasures, and gives you a slight edge in situations that are at all threatening: there are certain hours and certain precincts of the city in which a backup, even if the support is no more than moral, has real value. The drawback is that at times each of you will have your own agenda, and at times you'll be fed up with each other.

Solution: split up until your energy and interests are compatible again. New York is full of unexpected corners and odd adventures, and you'll find them more efficiently on your own.

Travelling in groups can be stifling for all concerned. If it can't be avoided, at least make sure that there are times when everyone gets to scout out the territory. For children especially the city is an incredible adventure, but the risks of turning them loose are not to be discounted. Your best bet when shepherding kids becomes too much a chore might be to let them do the leading: you'll most likely find yourselves in improbable, untouristed places.

Climate and timing your trip

If you have some choice in the matter – if your schedule is not dictated by company business or errands of mercy – the best time to be in New York is the autumn (known to Americans as the fall). Late September to the end of November is ideal, when the city comes alive after the summer doldrums. Second best is the spring – mid-April to the end of May. The height of summer and the depth of winter are a toss-up for last place: you should base your plans on whether you suffer more from bitter, knife-edge winds or paralysing heat and humidity, and schedule accordingly.

New York is 11 degrees of latitude south of London, and nowhere near as temperate: its winters are bitter cold, its summers hot and steamy. Unlike Paris and Los Angeles, the city doesn't lie in a basin and so tends not to suffer smog and heat build-up. Breathing is no problem. But surviving extremes of heat and cold is not easy, especially because Americans tend to combat summer and winter with megatons of air conditioning and central heating. Every transition you make from street to shelter, in the hot and cold seasons, is a shock to the system. You can faint from heat in the dead of winter or come down with chills in a hotel lobby in August. The only known preventive is sensible dress.

What to take

What you carry determines how easily and efficiently you move around, and it's always a good idea to take less than what you think you'll need. The season and the length of your stay will have something to do with what you take, and whether you plan to sit tight in New York or move around the country will make a difference in your packing. Some basic advice:

1 Dress in layers. Take clothes you can shed or don from moment to moment. Everything you have should be easily washable or dry-cleanable. A warm overcoat is essential in winter, but otherwise heavy items should be left at home. From March to May and from late October to December, a light, waterproof coat and a series of sweaters will see you through. In summer, you'll need light, airy clothes and a cool, carryable jacket.

2 New York is not a clean city. The air is no more laden with grime than any other prime real estate, but the surfaces you'll bump into and rub up against are layered with the residue of the Industrial Revolution; you will be, too, whether you like it or not. Solution: *wear dark clothes*. When push comes to shove, see Laundry, p.191.

3 Take a couple of pairs of sturdy, well broken-in shoes; for women, they should be of different heel heights. You'll spend most of your time in the city on foot, and if your feet give out you're sunk. New Yorkers (especially women) have taken to wearing running shoes – Nikes, Adidas and such – on the streets. They're an incongruous sight below skirts and suits, but eminently practical. Office workers carry dress shoes in a bag, a practice you might want to emulate.

4 Take nothing you haven't worn before, and nothing you don't love. If your clothes don't meet these specs, they're a waste of luggage space.

5 *Indispensables*:
A cotton kimono.
For cold weather, a really warm, soft scarf – wool for preference. And two identical pairs of gloves – lined in winter – because you're going to lose one glove the day you arrive.
Dual voltage blow-dryers and electric razors (see Electricity, p.187).
A plastic carrier-bag for unwashed clothes. A few plastic bags and twist-ties. A featherweight bag that folds into your luggage, and can double as an overnight case to carry home all the extras you will buy.
Nail scissors and, even more important, toenail clippers, which will keep you ambulatory.

Glasses or contacts if you wear them: take an extra pair and/or a recent prescription.

Drugs: an adequate supply, and a recent prescription.

Three or four lightweight plastic hangers for drip-drying. A few clip-type clothes pegs. A little detergent in a plastic squeeze bottle (see Laundry, p.191).

You can pick up a collapsible umbrella almost anywhere in the city – even at a newsstand – for about $4.00, so don't bother to carry one across the ocean.

All of this, excluding what you wear on your back, should fit into a fairly small suitcase that should travel as carry-on luggage, bypassing the baggage carousel at Kennedy or Newark Airport and speeding you through the Customs and Immigration lines. Take along a thin, strong, nylon soft-sac for *en route* essentials such as book, flask, camera, tissues, maps and whatever else it takes to get you across the Atlantic in one piece.

Money questions
How much to take?

(For denominations and mechanics, see Money, p.196.) Advance planning is essential. You'll have to work out for yourself what's important to you, and how much you can afford. Budget for your extravagance, and save somewhere else. New York is not a cheap town, and poverty has no romantic connotations there: you'll have to brace yourself for spending unspeakable sums on the smallest goods and services. But if seven million New Yorkers, not all of them millionaires, can stay afloat, so can you.

	Maximum	*Minimum*
Transport to and from New York	£2576.00 (Concorde)	£294.00 (PeoplExpress)
Hotel per night See pp.58–74 for details.	$305.00 (Plaza)	$40.00 (bed and breakfast)
Food per day	$50.00	$15.00
Getting around per day See pp.31–41 for details	$20.00 (taxis)	$2.00 (subways)

The sights	$20.00	$0.00
See pp.148–172 for details.		
The shops	no limit	$0.00
See pp.173–184 for details.		

Necessities

See pp.14–15 for details.

Emergencies

Maximum and minimum depend entirely on you, and upon circumstance. Whether you're accident-prone or not, provide extra money for crises.

Insurance

Health insurance is absolutely vital: getting seriously ill without major medical coverage is a good way to put your family in hock for generations to come. Don't skimp. Most travel insurance policies provide only £5–15,000 coverage. £50,000 is a more realistic figure. Grill your travel agent on the subject, or contact an insurance group that caters to travellers: Europ-Assistance, in Croydon, is one.

You might well want to take out property insurance as well. Contrary to popular belief, not everyone gets ripped off in New York, but if you're carrying anything of value you'll be more relaxed if you're insured.

How to carry money
Cash

To minimize the hassles of airport arrival, it's a good idea to carry enough cash in dollars to get you into the city and settled. Arm yourself with enough cash for a day or two. Change pounds to dollars before you leave home, at a bank or exchange bureau where you know you'll get a good rate.

Traveller's cheques

Buy traveller's cheques in dollars and you'll be able to use them for shopping, some meals, and lodging: but don't expect to pay for a cup of coffee with a $50 traveller's cheque. Traveller's cheques in pounds are trickier to cash – only banks and exchange bureaux will attempt it – and speculating on currency futures while the exchange rates fluctuate isn't the purpose of your trip. Your own bank may offer traveller's cheques as a free service (but avoid the lesser-known brands, which can be difficult to cash in some New York banks and won't work at all in shops). The most common brands are American Express and Bank of America. Thomas Cook, Barclay's and National Westminster won't be readily cashable in some stores and restaurants, but – apart from inevitable, interminable lines – no problem in banks. Foreign exchange offices are fewer on the ground, but less crowded. See p.197 for a sampling. Size of denominations depends on how often you care to sign your name, and how reckless you become when you've cashed a big one.

Eurocheques

These don't work in America. Some banks do have reciprocal deals with New York counterparts, and you might check to see whether yours can give you cheque-cashing privileges in the US.

Barclaycard (VISA), Access (Mastercard), Amex, Diners Club, etc.

Credit cards are rapidly becoming a substitute for cash, and they provide great insurance against the day you run out of the ready. Almost everyone in New York – other than the Mafia – accepts plastic. You'll find that restaurants often accept American Express and Diners Club cards, but VISA and Access/Mastercard rarely. And note: the exchange rate at which you are billed is calculated by the issuing company on the day they bill you, not the day you used the card, so you can't know in advance how much you are spending. If you plan to use credit cards constantly, you'll have to balance the pros of waiting out the billing cycle against the cons of forking out interest. You should also be aware of your own threshhold of temptation. A little plastic is a dangerous thing.

Booking hotels in advance

If you know what you want, where you want to be, and how much you want to pay (see Housing, pp.58–78), it's *essential* to reserve several weeks in advance. It can save you energy and anxiety when you're just off the plane, staggering with jet-lag. And it can save you money: if you arrive to find your first choices booked up, you're likely to stumble into a hotel you can't afford (or can't tolerate) out of pure desperation. If you've made reservations and find yourself in a hotel you don't like, it's a lot easier to seek out another on a bedside telephone than from a phone booth in Grand Central Station.

Most hotels will require a deposit for the first night's stay. A traveller's cheque or an international money order, available at the post office, will take care of it. Or you can phone in your American Express card number (but not VISA or Mastercard/Access).

Getting there

The basic choices are simple: sea or air. We'll save the sea routes for a small paragraph later; airfares are a far more challenging subject. If you can find a travel agent who's willing to spend some time and effort on you, you're home free.

Flights
Discounts, charters, special tickets

Commercial flights to the US are available at widely varying prices – in 1985, major ticket agents began to handle discounted fares in a quiet way. They won't volunteer the information, but you can book PeoplExpress and Virgin Atlantic through, among others, Thomas Cook. All agents also offer the standard fares (APEX) of big airlines, the catch being that you have to book 21 days in advance and book your return flight at the same time. Standby fares came back in '85, for off-season travel: British Airways cut its one-way winter standby to New York to £149, £30 cheaper than its normal standby, to come close to PeoplExpress's fare of £147 plus food. The BA cheapie was of course for a limited time; tickets could be bought in advance but actual booking confirmation was only possible on the day of travel. Some travel agents can offer last-minute seats on transatlantic flights without the 21-day wait: among them, Trailfinders, 46 Earls Court Road, London W8 (tel: 01–937–9631). Shop around. Look at the back pages of *Time Out*, London's alternative magazine. Remember that agents who belong to ABTA (Association of British Travel Agents) can bail you out if the airline or charter group goes bust, while bucket shops can't. Don't part with the entire fare until the ticket is in your hand.

PeoplExpress is New Jersey's revisionist version of Laker's Folly, and so far it works. Five flights a week from Gatwick to Newark Airport (just across the Hudson from Manhattan). No frills – you pay for meals and checked luggage, cabin luggage allowance is only 5 kilos – but a lot of pride, as all employees are shareholders and everyone (apart from pilots and mechanics) does everything from booking flights to stowing luggage. Cheap, efficient, friendly, with a devoted following. High season fares in 1985 were about £169 each way, dropping £20 in September and October, and slightly lower in mid-winter. Available through IATA travel agents, or direct from CP Air Holidays, Cross Key's House, Haslett Avenue, Crawley, Sussex. Telephone: 0293–38100.

Virgin Atlantic fares are roughly the same as PeoplExpress, Gatwick–Newark, but they include food, soft drinks and sometimes on-board live entertainment, which can be slightly bizarre. From IATA travel agents or direct at Virgin record shops in London.

For up-to-the-minute information on best buys transatlantic, call the Air Travel Advisory Board, 01–636–5000, who will give you the numbers of several travel agents offering good deals.

Charter flights are not to be despised. Their advantage is that they're cheap. The disadvantage is that they must be booked at least two months in advance, and once booked they're ironclad. You can't have second thoughts without losing money. If you're booking a charter flight, make sure that whoever you buy it from has an Air Travel Organizer's Licence: a sort of financial pedigree from the Civil Aviation Authority.

Airpasses not only get you across the Atlantic but allow you to knock around the States for a given length of time and are available through major US airlines. They're generally good for 60 or 90 days, and anywhere from four to twelve stops. In most cases, you have to arrange your itinerary in advance . . . but it's a cheap and efficient way to visit all your cousins.

Open-jaw routes: For many New Yorkers, the city is all they know and all they need to know about America. This may not be true for you. You might want to fly from London to New York, travel around the country for a bit, and return home via San Francisco or Vancouver or any city with an international airport.

Baggage allowances

For economy seats, it's two pieces of luggage, one of which is no bigger than 65 inches (length + width + height), and the other no more than 55 inches. Excess baggage charges are another argument for travelling light. If you do find yourself at the check-in desk with excess baggage, try to find a sympathetic, underburdened soul who's willing to pool luggage with you.

Flight survival

There's an art to getting off a plane in one piece and with minimal jet-lag:

1 Fly at odd hours, off-season, and hope for an empty plane. If you have three seats to yourself you can swing the centre armrests up and stretch out. Ask for a window-seat, so that you can lean up against the side.
2 There are usually thin blankets and petite pillows in the overhead compartment. You can use them to fool yourself into sleeping.
3 Drink as much as you can on the plane – but no coffee and no alcohol. The stewards and stewardesses will fill you with as much 7-Up and Coke as you can hold, but something non-fizzy (water) is a better bet, and there are fountains with minuscule cups at strategic locations. The point is to re-hydrate yourself: the recycled air drains your system, and if you replace what you lose, you won't be such a wreck when they decant you from the plane.
4 If you're not actually asleep, it's a good idea to get up and walk around the plane as often as possible, stretch, do exercises – whatever it takes to keep your blood running and your muscles from bunching.
5 For psychological conditioning, set your watch to destination-time when you get on the plane.

Lost luggage

If your luggage doesn't turn up on the carousel at Kennedy, don't leave the airport without reporting it. First, find the lost-luggage office and see if the officials there can locate your bags. If they turn up on some other flight, the airline will have them sent to you. If not, they'll give you a form to fill out. Hang on to your airline ticket, the baggage-claim tags attached thereto, and your copy of the lost-property report. You're now on the road to compensation.

Sea routes

The one absolute cure for jet-lag is to travel by sea. If you have an extra week or so to kill, lots of luggage, plenty of money, and an aptitude for shuffleboard, it's ideal. Plus you can catch up on Tolstoy.

Entrances and exits

Passports, visas, customs

You'll need a valid passport to enter the US. In Britain, standard passports are good for ten years, and cost £15. Get forms from your local post office. Two photographs are needed. Return the application, with fee and photos, countersigned by someone impressive who knows you – vicar, solicitor, doctor or JP – either to the passport office or to the nearest main post office in your city. Expect to wait about ten days for the passport in winter, or up to a month in peak periods. Don't leave it till the last minute.

A British Visitor's Passport – the kind that's good for one year only – is not valid for travel to the US.

Visas and length of stay

Despite the welcoming words engraved on the Statue of Liberty in New York Harbor ('Give me your tired, your poor, your huddled masses . . .'), the US Department of Immigration and Naturalization is less than all-embracing. If you're a full-time student or university exchange visitor, or if you're planning to work in the US, you'll need to make arrangements for the appropriate visa well in advance. Your employer or university will usually start the ball rolling.

For a visitor's visa, you can either queue up at the Embassy in London (between 8.00 a.m. and 3.00 p.m.) or apply through your travel agent several weeks before you plan to travel. In either case, you'll need to submit your passport, a passport-sized photo, a stamped, addressed envelope and some proof that your visit will be temporary – six months maximum. The whole exercise is aimed at keeping you from threatening the job security of the American worker. For details, enquire at the US Embassy (Visa Branch, 5 Upper Grosvenor Street, London W1: 01–499–3443 for a recorded message, or 01–499–7010 for a human being).

Customs

US Customs officials are no more and no less rigorous than their British and Continental colleagues. What slows the process down is the lack of a 'wave-on' area. The system is like a supermarket checkout line, so it's impossible to breeze through it. The Customs officials are very curious about items like drugs, explosives, firearms, alcohol and fresh food (the Department of Agriculture frowns on unlicensed imports).

Duty-free allowances

200 cigarettes, 50 cigars or 2 kilos of tobacco
1 litre of alcohol
'Gifts' up to $100 in value

There are duty-free shops on the departure side of airports, but if you're travelling late these shops may be closed. Payment is in cash or credit cards.

Arriving

Kennedy Airport ('JFK' for short) is like any other airport, but more spread out than most. Some recent rulings have lessened the time your plane spends waiting for permission to land or take off, but the airport experience is at once stultifying and fraught with anxiety, and you should try to get it over with as quickly as possible. If you travel with carry-on luggage only, you'll eliminate the wait at the baggage carousel, and any possibility of lost luggage.

If you're travelling without enough dollars to get you through the next day or so, it would be a good idea to exchange pounds for dollars before you leave the airport. You'll find an exchange booth at the International Arrivals Building, open all the year round 8.00 a.m.–9.30 a.m., seven days a week. American money: see p.196.

Once you're through the formalities of arrival, it's a question of finding your way into Manhattan (Kennedy is due east of the city, in the borough of Queens). No matter how you travel, it's going to take at least an hour.

The Carey Bus System: This is my personal favourite because it's cheap, direct and relatively painless. The drawback is that it has to fight traffic. Bus drivers have claimed to make it in thirty minutes, and they have also admitted to 2½ hours. The cost is $8.00 one way, $13.00 round trip. Tickets are sold at the Carey desk at the airport exit (or you can pay the driver when you board); then it's out the door and sit on your luggage till the bus arrives. The interval between buses is about half an hour in the mornings and late evenings, 15 minutes between noon and 8 p.m. The destination from Kennedy is Grand Central Station (actually Park Avenue and 42nd Street, just across the street), and there's a shuttle bus from Grand Central to the Port Authority Bus Terminal, 44th Street and Eighth Avenue. The Grand Central area is infinitely more pleasant, but the Port Authority stop is convenient if your ultimate destination is on the west side of the city.

Taxis and limousines: Can be shared with other travellers and will take you to your door, but they're expensive and they have to fight the same traffic as buses. Taxis are yellow and more often than not fairly decrepit. Limousines are generally black and enormous, and will cost you plenty unless you team up with others on their way into town: it's perfectly kosher to split a cab or a limo (about $30.00 from Kennedy to midtown) with others on their way in, and it's economical if you and your fellow-travellers are bound for the same neighbourhood. Check the price with the driver in advance: there are horror stories of newcomers to the city, especially obvious foreigners, paying up to $100.00 for the trip. The phrase 'being taken for a ride' probably originated at Kennedy. See p.38 for more on taxis.

The Train to the Plane: A New York Transit Authority innovation. You board an 'Express Bus' from the airport to the Howard Beach/JFK Airport stop on the Eighth Avenue-IND Subway (more about subways on p.34). From there, it's a fast (but not scenic) subway ride into town. The cost is $6.10: a $1.00 subway token to board the train, and $5.10 collected once you're aboard. Trains run about every 20 minutes. The train makes no stops till Jay Street/Borough Hall, in Brooklyn, then on to Broadway/Nassau Street, in Manhattan, West 4th Street, 34th Street, 42nd Street,

Rockefeller Center and 57th Street. You can change trains at any of these stations and, with ingenuity, find your way underground to where you're staying. With luggage and a case of jet-lag, it can make you want to turn around and get back on the plane.

You can also take a **helicopter** into the city. If you can afford a ride in a helicopter, you really shouldn't be reading this book.

If you travel by bus or cab, your first view of New York will be of its suburban freeways, increasingly congested as you approach the city, and the landscape increasingly industrial. The reward for keeping your eyes open through all this is a staggering glimpse of the Manhattan skyline, followed by the Queens-Midtown Tunnel and the city itself.

From **Newark Airport**, west of Manhattan on the other side of the Hudson, most of the above applies except:

1 There's no 'Train to the Plane.'
2 The Carey buses take you to the Port Authority Terminal; from there you can continue on to Grand Central if you wish.
3 Taxi fares into the city from New Jersey are prohibitively high – about $30 – because of interstate regulations.

The Newark airport is smaller and somehow more hospitable than Kennedy, and it's a marginally quicker ride into town . . . but few international flights (other than PeoplExpress and Virgin) arrive there.

Before you find yourself on the street: You will have gathered, from the bus ride in, that traffic in the US travels on the right-hand side of the road. Although most traffic in New York runs on one-way streets, it will save your life if you remember to LOOK LEFT when you're crossing the street.

From Grand Central Terminal (42nd Street and Park Avenue) the bus deposits you on the sidewalk on the East side of Park Avenue, at the corner of 42nd Street. It's a busy intersection, but if you're not in any rush you should collect yourself and try to get your bearings. The direction in which the bus is facing as it lets you off is *north*. With some exceptions the avenues of Manhattan run north and south – uptown and downtown – and the streets east/west. Directly to your north, across 42nd Street, is Grand Central Station. If you feel like an immediate glimpse of the city, you can cross the street and check your bags in Grand Central –

but lockers are few, and to unload your luggage in the checkroom means waiting in line when you leave it and again when you pick it up. Your best bet now is to take a cab to your destination: don't mess with the subways until you're ready for adventure. If your hotel or apartment is on the west side of town, you'll want to cross 42nd Street and hail a cab heading west; if you're going east, stay on the downtown (south) side of 42nd Street. All taxis are yellow, and vacant ones have lit signs on top. See p.202 for information on rates and tipping.

From Port Authority Terminal (42nd Street and Eighth Avenue) you're dropped indoors in the northwest corner, ground floor, of the terminal. It's not the kind of place you'll want to spend much time in: crowded and impersonal. Nor is it any use trying to park your baggage and go for a stroll. There are only three banks of left-luggage lockers in the terminal, and they're all invariably full. In the terminal's south building, behind the Trailways Bus desks, there's a luggage checkroom, possibly the least efficient one in the Western world, and with the longest lines. The Port Authority neighbourhood is anything but picturesque, and doesn't invite a casual peruse, so your immediate priority will probably be to head for your hotel: by taxi, unless you can't bear to stay out of the subway. Make your way to the Eighth Avenue exit of the terminal and flag down a cab.

If you are ready to brave the New York subway and bus systems, see pp.34–37, 'Getting Around'.

Help
The Travelers' Aid Society

Service desk at JFK: 718–656–4870
207 West 43rd Street: 944–0013
and

Travelers' Aid Society of New York

2 Lafayette Street: 577–7700

For emergencies. Help for non-residents who are stranded or crime victims, provided by the New York Department of Social Services.

New York Convention and Visitors' Bureau

2 Columbus Circle: 397–8222

For information about the city sights and events, and if you're stuck, they'll give you a hand in finding a hotel.

Leaving

Don't forget to confirm your return flight reservation at least 72 hours before takeoff. A phone call to the airline takes care of it.

If you're heading straight home, apply all the above in reverse: taxi to Grand Central or Port Authority (or subway if you're not too heavily laden), and Carey bus to JFK or Newark; or some combination of subways that puts you on the Train to the Plane. Allow plenty of time. You can be pretty sure that it will be raining when you leave, or rush-hour, and every New York cab driver will be off duty; that the bus will be gridlocked before you get off 42nd Street; that the subway will stall on the tracks. Make ample allowance for this.

If you're travelling elsewhere: as long as you're on the left-hand side of the Atlantic, how about Boston, Chicago, San Francisco, New Orleans? Key Largo, Saranac, Santa Fe, Nantucket, the Carolinas and the Dakotas?

By plane: innumerable airlines serve New York, via three airports: Kennedy, LaGuardia and Newark. Of the three, LaGuardia is the most convenient, though Newark is just as close – only slightly more expensive to get to, because you must cross the state line into New Jersey on the way, which for some reason affects the fare. The mechanics of getting a good deal on a flight are known only to travel agents and their computers. Most are perfectly trustworthy, but some work harder than others to fit your needs. Use the Yellow Pages of the phone book to find one with an office near you, or – better still – get a recommendation from a New York acquaintance.

PeoplExpress is the no-frills favourite for do-it-yourself budget travel. You book your reservation directly with the airline (which can mean a long wait on the phone). Except for the Newark-Gatwick run, it's classless, and fares are based on peak (Monday-Friday, 7.00 a.m.–7.00 p.m.) and off-peak fly-times. So far its routes

are fairly short-haul – nothing much farther west than the Mississippi – and, apart from Boston and Washington, the destinations are a bit off the beaten track: places like Norfolk, Virginia, and Burlington, Vermont. But who wants to be on the beaten track?
PeoplExpress
North Terminal, Newark Airport
Newark, NJ 07114
201–596–6000

By train: Amtrak has long been America's excuse for a railroad, though it's said to be improving. It's still possible to see the country by rail, though you'd be better off flying to Montreal and taking the trans-Canada train. The passenger cars are few, the tracks ill-maintained, the once-magnificent stations in disrepair, and the trains late. But if you're heading upstate, or to Boston and New England, and if you can manage to see out of the windows, it might be worth your while for the view. If you're travelling long distances by rail, you must reserve well in advance.

The Long Island Railroad terminus is at Pennsylvania Station, 34th Street and Eighth Avenue. Trains run east through Queens to Long Island's beaches and bedroom communities. Unless you have friends with houses in the Hamptons, there's not much point in boarding. Some numbers:
Amtrak: 736–4545
Long Island Railroad: 718–739–4200

By bus: Greyhound and Trailways are the heavy haulers: they travel everywhere, cheaply and on time. They're long on economy and short on comfort and style, but you do manage to see the country – all of it, if you want. A major disadvantage is the rest stops: pitiful terminals inevitably located in the most run-down part of every town, gathering-places for local disreputables. Both lines run from the Port Authority Terminal, 44th Street and Eighth Avenue. For fare and schedule information:
Greyhound Bus Lines: 635–0800
Trailways: 730–7460

There are also lots of specialized services – Adirondack Trailways, for upstate New York; Bonanza, for Connecticut; Liberty and others, for the Atlantic City casinos. They're all in the Yellow Pages under 'Buses'.

By car: The major nationwide rental chains are Avis, Budget, Hertz and National: convenient if you want to travel one-way and leave your car in another city. Local rental companies may be cheaper, but may not give you the option of ditching the car out of town. Everyone has discounts: special overnight, daily, weekend, weekly and/or monthly rates; rates with or without mileage charges and drop charges; free pick-up service; and so on. The newest wrinkle is 'rent-a-wreck' – supercheap rates for driveable but less than pristine vehicles. You can also rent a Rolls, a Jeep, or anything in between. It's all in the Yellow Pages. See p.203 for cautionary words on driving.

Getting around town

Of the five boroughs of New York City, you'll spend virtually all your time on Manhattan, which, luckily for your feet, is a fairly small island. If high-speed tourism appeals to you, you can take a brisk walk from the Battery to Harlem, zigzagging around town, with stops at major attractions, in less than a day. On the other hand, an afternoon at the Metropolitan Museum can put you in a wheelchair. It's a matter of pace and energy and knowing your way around. Your first duty to your feet is to equip yourself with a map.

Maps

The most convenient set of maps I know is the Flashmaps Instant Guide to New York: clear, comprehensive, and portable. Unlike the London 'A-Z' atlas or the Leconte 'Plan de Paris', it's not a detailed, indexed compendium but an overview of the city, with theatres, hotels, restaurants, art galleries, consulates, parks, hospitals and such flagged on separate pages and an invaluable address-finder (how else are you to know that 350 Fifth Avenue – the Empire State Building – is located between 33rd and 34th Streets?). There are detailed maps of Lincoln Center (the music/dance/opera complex), Central Park, the United Nations, and the labyrinth of streets in lower Manhattan. There are seating maps of the sports arenas, a geological map, and a breakdown of the island by neighbourhood. And seven pages of bus and subway maps which are even clearer than those the New York City Transit Authority* puts

---

* If you do want 'official' bus and subway maps, which are quite beautiful, you can find them – free – at the Metropolitan Transportation Authority

out. All for $3.95, and available at most bookstores.

You'll also find excellent colour maps in the American Express Pocket Guide to New York, and in the familiar Michelin guide – the tall, green paperback edition, whose only drawback is that it sticks out of your pocket like a flag marked 'Tourist!' The New York Convention and Visitors' Bureau, which has its own circular tower in Columbus Circle (southwest corner of Central Park), gives away a not very detailed fold-out map of the city, along with armloads of brochures – and flyers on seasonal events and permanent attractions around town. Or you can pick up an ordinary fold-out street map – Rand McNally or some such, accurate to the last alley and about the size of a small tablecloth, but don't try to read it on the subway at rush hour.

Geography lesson

New York City consists of five boroughs: Brooklyn, the Bronx, Queens, Staten Island and Manhattan. Unless you're an ardent explorer or have relatives in 'the boroughs', you can consign all but the island of Manhattan to oblivion. Naturally there are exceptions to this harsh rule, and we'll discuss some of them elsewhere. For now, what you need to know is that Manhattan is an island, about thirteen miles long from north to south and two miles wide, bounded by the Hudson River on the west and by the East River, you guessed it, on the east. Anything north of you is 'uptown', and anything to the south 'downtown'. If you're travelling east or west, you're going 'crosstown'.

The Streets and Avenues

Manhattan was settled from the bottom up. The southern tip of the island – Lower Manhattan – is a tangle of streets left over from the Dutch colonization. They have names rather than numbers, and a pronounced un-American tendency to twist and turn, but gradually

---

headquarters at 347 Madison Avenue, between 44th and 45th Streets. They're buried in the basement, so you'll have to ask at the lobby desk for directions. Or write to the New York City Transit Authority, 370 Jay Street, Brooklyn, NY 11201. The subway map covers all boroughs; for bus maps, be specific.

they conform to the uptown grid pattern as they move north. Apart from the maze of lower Manhattan, the city runs on a strict checkerboard pattern of numbered streets from Washington Square north to the Harlem River.

The numbered streets run east and west, like ribs along the central stem of Fifth Avenue: everything east of Fifth is on the 'East Side', everything west is on the 'West Side'. The farther north – or 'uptown' – the higher the street number.

The avenues run north and south, beginning with York Avenue at the East River, and continuing west toward the Hudson with First, Second, Third, Lexington, Park, Madison, Fifth and Sixth Avenues, and so forth to Twelfth Avenue, with notable exceptions. The exceptions:

Broadway – an eccentric aunt to all the other avenues. Runs north from Battery Park, tilts westward at 8th Street, crosses Fifth Avenue into the West Side at 23rd Street, and continues to angle westward until it hits 79th Street, at which point it continues north again. To make matters worse, there's also a northbound street in Lower Manhattan called West Broadway, which parallels the real Broadway for a few blocks. Each time Broadway crosses another avenue it forms a 'square' or a 'circle': Union Square (Park Avenue), Madison Square (Fifth), Herald Square (Sixth), Times Square (Seventh), Columbus Circle (Eighth).

Between **Hudson Street** on the south and **14th Street** on the north, there are an extra four avenues where the island juts into the East River: Avenues A, B, C and D.

Fourth Avenue – more or less parallels lower Broadway, then peters out at Union Square (14th Street), where Park Avenue begins.

Sixth Avenue – renamed 'Avenue of the Americas' some years ago, but no native has ever called it that. Becomes Lenox Avenue north of Central Park.

Seventh Avenue – in its passage through the Garment District (between 28th and 38th Streets) it's called (but the words have never graced the air) 'Fashion Avenue', and north of Central Park it's known as Adam Clayton Powell, Jr. Boulevard.

Eighth Avenue – becomes Central Park West at 59th Street, and resumes its former identity at 110th Street.

Ninth Avenue – becomes Columbus Avenue at 59th Street, and then becomes Morningside Drive at 110th Street.

Tenth Avenue – becomes Amsterdam Avenue at 59th Street.

Eleventh Avenue – becomes West End Avenue at 59th Street, and merges with Broadway at 110th Street. Fifty-ninth Street itself becomes Central Park South at the base of the park, and 110th Street is Cathedral Parkway from the Hudson east to Eighth Avenue (aka Columbus), when it becomes Central Park North.

In other words, a simple grid pattern, with as many oddities as the English language has irregular verbs. In spite of everything, it's impossible to get lost in New York if you can orient yourself toward the north. And there are enough clearly visible landmarks – the Empire State Building and the World Trade Center, among others – to give you clues to your whereabouts.

The standard unit of distance measurement in New York is the 'block'. Keep in mind that there are 'short' blocks and 'long' blocks in Manhattan: the blocks running east and west, between the avenues, are generally about three times as long as those running north and south, between the streets. A stroll across town – a mere twelve blocks – will take you as long as a 40-block hike up or downtown.

The Subway

Not a subterranean passage but an underground railway. New York's rotting subway system is unparalleled for grime, poor signage, vandalism, hooliganism, sheer decibels and general nefariousness. But it gets you there – quickly, if not in style. The graffiti alone are mind-boggling: they range from crude, indecipherable trademarks on the interior walls (and seats and ceilings) of the cars to technicolor extravaganzas on the exteriors.

The subways consist of three basic lines, all owned by the city: the IRT (Interborough Rapid Transit), the IND (Independent Subway System), and the BMT (Brooklyn–Manhattan Transit). Each line runs local trains, which make all stops, and express trains which have their own tracks and shoot past the less significant stations.

The **IRT** has two major routes: the Broadway–Seventh Avenue

line, which runs north and south under the West Side (the Nos. 1, 2 and 3 trains), and the Lexington Avenue line, which runs north and south under the East Side (the Nos. 4, 5 and 6). These are connected by a 'shuttle', which runs under 42nd Street between Times Square and Grand Central Station.

The **IND** runs trains parallel to the IRT West Side operation, under Eighth Avenue and Central Park West (the A and AA trains), and offshoots that serve the Lower East Side (the B, D and F trains) and Queens, via midtown (the E and F trains).

The **BMT** consists of a crosstown train, the LL, which runs east along 14th Street from Eighth Avenue to Brooklyn; another along 57th and 59th Street from Sixth Avenue to Queens (the RR); and a third, the J train, which runs from Broad Street, in the financial district, north through the Lower East Side to Brooklyn.

If this sounds complex on paper, wait till you see it in real life. There is an almost total absence of maps in the subway stations – occasionally you'll find one outside the turnstiles, but never near the tracks, where you need them, and in the subway cars themselves they've generally been obliterated by graffiti. There are directional signs, but they're often cryptic: the only indication of the existence of the Times Square–Grand Central shuttle, for instance, is the letter 'S' on a few girders. In many stations, trains are referred to by number or letter only – not route or destination. You'll have to take your chances and ask directions – or carry a map.

The only people in New York who seem to have subway passes are schoolchildren and MTA employees. Everyone else (apart from hooligans, who leap the turnstiles) uses 'tokens' – brass coins the size of a quarter,* which cost $1.00 each. You can buy them at the glassed-in booths at each station, and it'll save you time if you buy them in quantity – in packets of ten. Deposit your token in the slot on top of the turnstile before you go through; then follow the signs, if any, to the appropriate track. A ride on the subway costs one token whether you travel one stop or all over town.

Subway etiquette, if it exists, amounts to minding your own business. Since the advent of the Sony Walkman and its clones, fewer people carry audible radios (audible is an understatement; the technical term is blasters) and in recent years the cars and stations are better patrolled by city and transit police. It's still a good idea to stand well away from the platform edge, especially in crowds, and to keep your wits about you generally. The subways run 24 hours a day, but not on all routes: 6.00 a.m. to midnight is the standard. Subway travel in the middle of the night may be hazardous to your health. If you must ride the trains after 10 or 11 at night, remember the following:
Stay in the best-lit part of the station, closest to the token booth.
Don't wander away from other people.
Try not to travel alone.
Board cars that have other people in them.
Switch cars if need be; one of them generally contains a transit cop.

For specifics on which trains run during the small hours, call 718–330–1234.

City buses

Manhattan buses travel on fifteen avenue routes and sixteen crosstown routes. Since most avenues are one-way, buses tend to make loops: uptown on Fifth Avenue and downtown on Madison; uptown on Third and downtown on Lexington; up on Tenth, down on Ninth; up on Sixth, down on Fifth: but both ways on Broadway, eccentric as ever.

Crosstown buses run on major crosstown streets: Grand Street,

* See Money, p.196.

Houston Street, 14th, 23rd, 34th, 42nd and 57th Streets, Central Park South and through Central Park at 66th/67th, 79th, 86th and 96th Streets. For best results, get a copy of the official MTA Manhattan Bus Map (see footnote on p.31), or use the Flashmaps guide (p.193).

Buses cost the same as subways: $1.00 per ride, regardless of distance. You'll need *exact change* in quarters, dimes and nickels, or (more convenient) a subway token. Enter the bus at a bus stop (clearly marked, and quite often sheltered from the elements) and toss your token or your money in the coin-collector at the driver's side, and find a seat or something to hang on to. There's a bell cord above you, or a pressure-sensitive strip along the windows in the newer buses: use these to signal the driver when you want to get off; you can leave the bus through the front or rear doors. All stops are request stops: if no one's outside waiting for a bus, and no one signals to get off, the driver won't stop.

If you want to transfer between avenue and crosstown buses, or get off for a bit and continue your ride later, you can ask the driver for a 'transfer' as you board your bus. These are free, time-validated, and won't work as return tickets, but they're useful nonetheless. For some reason, people are beginning to call transfers 'add-a-rides' (sounds slightly chemical?), but drivers still respond to the phrase, 'Transfer, please.'

Most buses run from 7.00 a.m. to 10.00 p.m., seven days a week, but there's 24-hour service on some of the more popular routes. For 24-hour bus and subway information, call 718–330–1234.

Standards of courtesy are far higher on buses than in subways. Passengers have been known to speak to each other and even to thank the driver as they get off; grown men have been seen to give up their seats to elderly women. On a recent trip across town on 86th Street, when most of the passengers got off at Madison Avenue, the driver called out, 'I'd like to wish each and every one of you a very nice day, and may God go with you on your way.' Gasps of disbelief.

Bus transport is subject to the whims of traffic – it's not uncommon to get wedged – and quite often you can travel faster on foot. But it does provide great opportunities for sightseeing and eavesdropping. Most New Yorkers are highly verbal – for Americans – and never more so than when they're barrelling down Fifth Avenue after a hard day of shopping.

The Transit Authority runs a couple of 'Express' buses – the X23 and the X25 – which run to and from Wall Street (the financial district) at rush hour: something to avoid at all costs.

The New York taxi

Two things in life are absolute: in Venice, gondolas are black, and in New York, legitimate taxis are yellow. The city swarms with taxis except when you need them most – it's a fact of life in New York that you can never find a cab in the rain; the same holds true for rush hour (7.30 to 9.30 in the morning, 5.00 to 7.00 at night).

An average taxi ride will cost you between $2 and $4, plus tip: a wild extravagance until the inevitable moment when you're desperate for a cab. It's ninety in the shade – you've been wandering through increasingly *louche* precincts and now you're utterly lost – your feet are worn to nubs – you can't even find the subway, much less face it. All you want is the most direct route to your room. Along comes your saviour – all you have to do is flag him down.

The rates for 'legit' New York taxis are $1.10 for the first ninth of a mile and 10 cents for each additional ninth of a mile. The meter starts running as soon as you get in. You can scoot up and down the avenues in no time, catching the lights, but keep in mind that crosstown trips, with constant traffic backups, are inevitably longer, more expensive and exasperating.

The rates are for distance, not number of passengers – but there's a fifty-cent extra charge for a fifth passenger, for trips made between 8.00 p.m. and 6.00 a.m., and for extra luggage – and for each 45 seconds of 'waiting time' (in traffic, at stop lights . . .) it'll cost you ten cents. It doesn't hurt to split a cab with acquaintances if you're heading the same way: sometimes it's marginally cheaper than the subway, but not always faster.

A standard tip is 15 per cent of the meter reading: more for a particularly delightful ride, less for an unusually harrowing one or a sullen driver. New York's cab drivers – those who speak English at all – have earned a reputation as 'characters' with big mouths, opinions on everything, full-blown philosophies which they will share with you in the space of a few blocks, and choice expletives for anything that obstructs their trajectories.

The exception to the yellow-cab rule is 'gypsy' cabs – almost indistinguishable from mainstream traffic, meterless, and unregulated (or inspected for safety) by the New York Taxi and Limousine Commission. Gypsies are technically not allowed to 'cruise' for passengers, and while travelling by gypsy doesn't automatically mean highway robbery, you have no recourse if you're ripped off.

You negotiate price when you enter the cab. This might be as simple as the driver saying, 'Pay what it usually costs.' The price should, in fact, be slightly less than the legitimate rate: it's black market transport, after all.

You'll find that legitimate 'medallion' cabs generally won't travel above 110th Street (the southern border of Harlem), and gypsies generally don't pick up passengers below 96th Street: a matter of established territory. Note also that the term 'gypsy' has nothing to do with the ethnicity of the driver — it means only that the cabs have no home base.

Radio cabs

Conventional wisdom is that radio cabs won't pick you up unless you've already got an 'in' with them. But it doesn't hurt to try. A few possibilities:

Bell Radio Taxi: 691–9191
Big Z: 718–445–8888
Fone-a-Cab: 718–706–0333

These are medallion cabs and are not allowed to charge more than metered fare. If you use one of the non-medallion 'Limousine' services, you'll have to negotiate a flat rate for your destination. They're listed under 'Car Svce.' and 'Taxicab Svce.' in the Yellow Pages. In any case, call well before you plan to leave. Radio cabs are legally bound to pick up anyone who flags them down on the way to you, but some have roof-lights that read 'on radio', and others switch on their 'off duty' lights to avoid interception.

New York on two wheels

The number of living bicyclists in Manhattan is surprising. Those who aren't hunted down by cab drivers (who despise them), those who survive suddenly-opened car doors and storm drains, and whose lungs aren't permanently saturated by exhaust, seem to delight in bike travel. It's definitely the fastest way to get around town. But even if you survive the ride, your bike may not survive the bicycle thieves, no matter how strong or elaborate your locks.

If your nerves are up to it, there are several agencies around town that rent bicycles. Among them:

Sixth Avenue Bicycles

546 Sixth Avenue (at 15th Street)
255–5100

Broadway Bicycle

92nd Street and Amsterdam Avenue
or 72nd Street Boathouse in Central Park
866–7600

Metro Bicycles

1311 Lexington Avenue (corner of 88th Street)
427–4450

Midtown Bicycles

360 West 47th Street (at Ninth Avenue)
581–4500

Rates are in the neighbourhood of $3.00 per hour, $15 per day. Some will hold your credit card hostage; others take a cash deposit – about $20.00.

Footwork

In Manhattan, as nowhere else in the United States, the pedestrian rules. For utter disdain of traffic laws, even taxis can't compete. Jaywalking has been developed to an art which pits the sheer gall of the pedestrian against the menace of traffic: rather like bullfighting. It's almost impossible to stay on the sidelines – you'll find yourself crossing against the lights, at midblock, in rush-hour traffic, without giving it a second thought: not because you're in a hurry, but because everyone else is. Sociological studies have proved that New Yorkers who obey traffic laws are suffering from severe depression.

The pace New Yorkers set is brisk. Everyone appears to be heading somewhere in a hurry. No one loafs or strolls, because the pedestrian tide won't permit it. There's little eye contact in the streets and little of the mutual appraisal between the sexes that goes on in more relaxed cities. You'll notice that New Yorkers tend to walk with their heads fixed forward, eyes focused on the middle distance – or even head down, eyes to the pavement – encapsulated in the crowds. A sociologist would probably diagnose extreme goal-orientation: it's the destination that counts, and getting there is something to have done with as fast as possible. Generally, if pedestrians acknowledge each other at all, it's over questions of right-of-way and territory: you'll see little eruptions of outrage and irritability on the sidewalks, incidents which flare up for a moment and flutter out immediately. Occasionally you'll find pedestrian life in New York a trifle raw, and in order to enjoy the streets it helps not to take superficial rudeness personally.

The racetrack quality of sidewalk traffic will do you in if you're not careful. You'll explore the city mostly on foot, and to keep your feet from giving out you'll have to consciously slow your pace – very difficult on busy streets – or take frequent rests. Among the possibilities are stops for meals, with intervening breaks for snacks or coffee; strategically placed public benches and low walls, especially in midtown (see Rest Stops, p.55); park benches (see Parks, p.148); non-rush hour transportation; museums and libraries; and as a last resort, the movies (see City Lights, p.131). Your best bet is to gauge your stamina and plan your outings accordingly, with enough stops along the way to stave off exhaustion.

The neighbourhoods

New York is a city of neighbourhoods – broad catch-all districts as well as tiny ethnic and cultural pockets. New Yorkers may pride themselves on cosmopolitan qualities, but they still orient themselves by neighbourhood.

You'll notice that the boundaries between neighbourhoods are very finely drawn: one block can make the difference between Chinese and Italian, finance and industry, slum and gentry. Sometimes the intimations of change in a neighbourhood can be spotted in a matter of months. New Yorkers are acutely sensitive to anything that affects the local turf. They'll form building associations, block associations, street gangs, neighbourhood watch groups, you name it – for better or worse, real estate is the most precious commodity in town.

Knowing where the neighbourhoods are and what they're about will make a big difference to your stay. They're distinct islands within an island, and you'll find you get more out of the city by exploring them individually. Here are some clues to what you'll find:

Lower Manhattan

This is the southern tip of the island, and where metropolitan life began in New York. For a heart-stopping immigrant's-eye-view of the city, take the Staten Island Ferry from Battery Park (cost: 25¢ outbound, free return). You don't have to get off at Staten Island – just turn around and see what welcomed America's waves of immigrants: the harbour, the Statue of Liberty, the burgeoning skyline. The city's oldest streets – Bridge Street, State Street, Whitehall, Pearl Street, Water Street – form a tangle at the foot of Manhattan. The widest of them was a Dutch canal, filled in to form

Broad Street at the end of the 17th century. A stroll north on Pearl or Water Streets and a left turn on Wall Street will take you into the financial district – the New York Stock Exchange (founded in the Tontine Coffee House, at the corner of Water Street) and Trinity Church, which nestles in among the skyscrapers like a rich little dowager. The parish still seems to own most of the land in lower Manhattan, though it divested itself of slum property in the 1890s.

Landmarks:
The World Trade Center: Below Vesey Street, at the edge of the Hudson. Twin towers of surpassing blandness. Since each is 110 stories tall, their virtue is that you can use them to orient yourself from almost any place in town. The view from the top is not at all bad.

The New York Stock Exchange: 8 Broad Street (between Wall Street and Exchange Place). It's the interior you want to see.

The Custom House: Whitehall (at Bowling Green). Turn-of-the-century Beaux Arts deluxe.

Civic Center

The area between City Hall Park and Foley Square is New York's Civic Center, a motley collection of architectural gems and excrescences. Best: City Hall itself, a scaled-down French renaissance palace; the Hall of Records, which has an authoritarian Napoleonic splendour of its own; the Municipal Building, a monumental pile straddling Chambers Street; the Woolworth Building, once the world's tallest, an imposing early-century Gothic 'Cathedral of Commerce'; and at the south end of the complex, St Paul's Chapel, late 18th-century, serene and dignified. City Hall Park itself was originally a common, planted with apple trees, and was the site of all sorts of civic celebrations and revolutionary commotions.

Landmark:
The Brooklyn Bridge: Pedestrian walkway begins at City Hall subway station, and ends at Cadman Plaza, in Brooklyn Heights (a delightful neighbourhood in its own right). If you're in the market for symbols and archetypes, nothing beats the towering, tapered granite buttresses of the Bridge and the supertension of its cable meshwork.

Chinatown

New York's Chinatown, like San Francisco's and Vancouver's, is a densely packed, bustling enclave, culturally isolated from the rest of the city. Even the banks are Chinese-owned and run. The neighbourhood has more food per square inch than any other part of town: groceries and outdoor stalls loaded with fresh seafood, exotic vegetables, obscure items smoked, dried, pressed, salted and otherwise preserved. Mott Street is the boulevard; Mulberry Street, Pell Street, Bayard Street and Doyers Street take up the overflow. Until about 1910, the intersection of Pell and Doyers was known as Bloody Angle, because so many tong wars culminated there. Despite

CORNER OF BROAD AND WALL STREETS—DREXEL'S BUILDING AND STOCK EXCHANGE.

its seething crowds and galvanic bursts of energy (especially at Chinese New Year, the first full moon after 21 January), the neighbourhood is still a mystery.

Lower East Side

Most of America's Irish immigrants passed through the Lower East Side during the famines of the 1850s. They were followed by waves of Germans, Italians, Greeks, Roumanians, Poles and Hungarians in the 1880s and, about the turn of the century, by an enormous influx of Jews, mostly from Russia, many of whose descendants are still here. Among their bequests are dozens of delicatessens, bakeries, kosher butcher shops and restaurants. The Jewish intelligentsia gathered in the cafés and theatres of Second Avenue in the early days of the century; the great political and social activists sprang out of the slums, along with anarchist and socialist newspapers; and those show-business geniuses who weren't actually brought up in the Jewish Rialto of the Lower East Side at least took their inspiration here. With the immigration quotas of the 1920s, the population dropped drastically; immense tracts of tenements were razed and replaced with 'projects', which house the multitudes antiseptically; and, except for the still-teeming markets of Essex and Orchard Streets, the streets are next to desolate.

Landmark:
The Henry Street Settlement: Henry Street, between Montgomery and Grand Streets. A row of 1820s townhouses distinguished by Anglophile architecture and a century of social service.

East Village

The former north end of the Lower East Side is now called the East Village, and its eastern frontier, Avenues A to D, 'Alphabet Land.' Until artists came in search of loft space, and actors for outlets, much of it was a burnt-out slum. It's still poor and beat-up and its eastern edge isn't particularly safe after dark, but it has lively pockets of creative endeavour. The inhabitants are a mixed bag:

fringe artists, a conclave of Hell's Angels on 3rd Street, first-generation Ukrainians on 7th, troupes of new- and no-wave types, and the inevitable uptown weekend curious. An invasion of chic is about to begin. If you keep your eyes open in the streets around Astor Place (the west edge of the East Village) – Lafayette Street, Bond Street, Great Jones Street – you'll find traces of New York's early 19th-century grandeur: the area was briefly the city's most fashionable district. A block away, the Bowery begins its 16-block run: flophouses for the city's detritus, interspersed with warehouses of commercial equipment. Bleak and wrenching, but an inextricable part of the city's fabric.

Landmarks:

Astor Place subway station: You can still make out the beaver motif among the tiles – it was the beaver hat that made John Jacob Astor's fortune.

Cooper Union: Cooper Square, just south of Astor Place. Heavy authoritarian brownstone – but a rich libertarian history.

Little Italy

There are dense pockets of Little Italy scattered throughout the territory from Canal Street north to Houston (pron. How-stun) Street, and from the Bowery west to Lafayette Street, with an annex in the streets just south of Washington Square. The red-brick residential streets of these neighbourhoods still have a Godfatherish texture – possibly because only the older generation, the last wave of actual immigrants, still remains. If you frequent the coffee houses and park benches of the Little Italies, you can't avoid overhearing hoarse Calabrian grandfathers picking over the life and times of the neighbourhood.

Landmarks:

The old **New York City Police headquarters:** 240 Center Street, between Grand and Broome. Redolent, overblown baroque.

Puck Building: 295 Lafayette Street, at Mulberry. Look up.

TriBeCa

TriBeCa – the *Tri*angle *Be*low *Ca*nal Street – is an old industrial quarter currently getting a facelift. A few years ago, it was overrun by rich artists; now it's full of 'co-op' loft apartments, elegant bars and restaurants, chic boutiques, a few hot galleries. Bounded by Chambers Street on the south, Broadway to the east, and the Hudson River on the west, and loaded with cast-iron facades: the 19th century's economical solution to a demand for exuberant architectural detail. White Street, Franklin Street, Leonard Street are among the best groomed, and West Broadway is becoming a handsome thoroughfare. The ancient warehouses loom above the streets – oddly serene at night. For an architectural about-face, check out the monolithic Western Union Building at Hudson and West Broadway: a 1930s masterpiece of brick.

SoHo

SoHo is an antique industrial district invaded by artists in the 1960s, who were followed immediately by hundreds of galleries (q.v. p.123). It's the area *so*uth of *Ho*uston, between Broadway and Varick Street. A profusion of cast-iron frontage: from leafy, whimsical and ornate to spartan, elegant and dignified. Mercer, Greene, and Wooster Streets are the stars of the neighbourhood, but even crass Broadway has its gems: the Singer Building, between Spring and Prince Streets, is a turn-of-the-century triumph of glass and steel – nonpareil commercial architecture. Canal Street, on SoHo's southern border, is a swarming bazaar of hardware shops, peddlers of gimcrackery and army-navy surplus outlets; but Houston Street, on the north, is a desolate wasteland barrier between SoHo and the Village.

Greenwich Village

Greenwich Village is universally known as the Village, and as the West Village to distinguish it from the East. Traditionally the artists' and writers' haven, and teeming with cafés, boîtes and tiny restaurants. Bounded on the east and west by Broadway and the

Hudson River, between West Houston Street and 14th Street, it encloses an illogical nest of streets west of Sixth Avenue, entirely appropriate for Bohemia. One of the few quarters of New York in which to *stroll*. Cummings, Dreiser, James, Melville, Millay, O'Neill, Poe, Thomas, Twain, Wharton, Whitman and a swarm of other knowns and unknowns spread among the last hundred years have lived, worked and played in the Village. Some of its districts have always been genteel: the Greek Revival houses along Washington Square North . . . the brownstone 'English Terrace' row on 10th Street, west of Fifth Avenue . . . the Federal houses scattered along Christopher Street, Gay Street, Grove Street . . . and those precincts that were once in any way seedy have now pretty much priced themselves out of the reach of starving artists.

Landmarks:

Jefferson Market: 10th Street and Sixth Avenue. A mammoth Victorian pile, complete with clocktower: once a courthouse, now a branch of the Library.

Washington Arch: At the north entrance of Washington Square Park: an 1890s monument to the Father of His Country.

Chelsea

Chelsea is a west side district constantly in turmoil, bounded west and east by the Hudson River and Fifth Avenue, and running from about 14th Street to 28th Street. Chelsea has seen everything from slaughterhouses to high society, and at various times has housed New York's theatre district, its artist colony, and its red-light district. Knots of interwoven commercial, industrial, borderline-slum and leafy residential streets – the neighbourhood will never be integrated, but it is coming up in the world. Most of the activity in Chelsea takes place on Eighth Avenue, in the upper 'teens: a raft of new and trendy restaurants signals the arrival of the young and affluent. The fashionable remains of turn-of-the-century Chelsea are clustered between 20th and 22nd Streets, around Tenth Avenue; the remains of its stylish department stores – Stern's, the original Altman's, and a row of block-long retail dry-goods stores – now serve as loft and office space on Sixth Avenue, in the lower 20s. The contrast between the brash discount commercialism of 23rd Street and the discreet Italianate townhouses a few blocks away will keep you guessing.

Landmark:
Chelsea Hotel: 222 West 23rd Street. Heavy brickwork refreshed by filigreed balconies. The ultimate Bohemian hotel.

Four Squares

The Four Squares – Union, Madison, Stuyvesant, Gramercy – started out on more or less equal footing a century ago, each with fond prospects of gentility. The only neighbourhood that kept its promise was **Gramercy Park** (Lexington Avenue, at 21st Street), to which some of New York's old money still clings: the opulent brownstones and dignified red-brick row houses surrounding the park, and the townhouses of Irving Place, were the headquarters of society's 'Four Hundred' in the Gilded Age. **Madison Square**, at the diagonal intersection of Fifth Avenue and Broadway at 23rd Street, has lost almost every vestige of glamour: Delmonico's, the original extravaganza of Madison Square Garden, and the old Fifth Avenue Hotel were the swells' gathering places, and are lost . . . but the area seems to be on the verge of a comeback. **Stuyvesant Square**, intersected by Second Avenue at 16th Street, has also seen better days; it now seems to be surrounded by hospitals. Two beauties: St George's Church, Gothic brownstone on Rutherford Place (west side of the Square), and the chaste Friends Meeting House, a block away. Around the corner, at 15th Street and Second Avenue, is the world's ugliest church, St Mary's (Byzantine Rite), a 1960s stained-glass and concrete eyesore. **Union Square** (diagonal intersection of Broadway and Fourth Avenue at 14th Street) became the soap-box oratory stage for New York's (and, by extension, America's) leftest of the left: the anarchists, the Wobblies, the once-thriving American Communist Party, held mass demonstrations, May Day parades and the occasional riot here. After a decade as a pushers' paradise, the park has just emerged from major refurbishment and promises to be drug-free for a while. The sleazy discount stores of 14th Street are ripe for demolition, and things are looking up in the neighbourhood.

Landmarks:
The Flatiron Building: 23rd Street, at the intersection of Broadway and Fifth Avenue. An elegant 21-story wedge, with the apex pointing north to Madison Square.

The Little Church around the Corner: A.k.a. Church of the Transfiguration, 1 East 29th Street. Sweet and petite. Beloved of theatre-folk since 1870, when it took on an actor's funeral refused by a nearby church.

The Players: 16 Gramercy Park South. Edwin Booth's elaborate brownstone club for New York's most adored minority, its actors.

Herald Square

The vicinity of Herald Square (the diagonal intersection of Broadway and Sixth Avenue, at 34th Street) is nothing much to look at, with the exception of the colossal General Post Office, on Eighth Avenue. There's also Macy's, for marathon shoppers; for sports fans, Madison Square Garden . . . and, to stretch the definition of the district, the Empire State Building, 34th Street and Fifth Avenue. (Yes, take the elevator to the top – nobody has to know you took this trite tourist jaunt. At midday in midsummer or in the dead of night in the dead of winter, the vista is without parallel.)

Garment District

Just to the north: the Garment District – Seventh Avenue, in the upper 30s – where life seems to run about 20 per cent faster than anywhere else on earth. You're as likely to be hit by a rack of dresses on wheels as by a taxi. Furs, flowers and clothes – manufacturers, wholesalers, discounters, hawkers – muddled together on all sides. Clamorous by day but pointless after dark.

Murray Hill

Murray Hill – Fifth Avenue to the East River, 24th Street to 42nd Street – is an old-fashioned residential district, with stately town-houses clustered among deco apartment buildings: the turf of *The New Yorker* magazine. The dormer windows of these elegant brownstones are likely to be outlined in oxidized copper, apple-green against grey slate, refreshing to the eye. The beginnings of lower

Park Avenue, polished, refined, are on a more human scale than its uptown end, where it's positively inspiring: at 42nd Street, it rises on ramps to the foot of Grand Central's elaborate Beaux Arts facade; statues of Mercury, Hercules, Minerva; stone, glass and steel. Eastward: Lexington Avenue, in the 30s, a curious mix of high-rise offices and tiny groceries, culminating at 42nd Street with the miraculous deco tower of the Chrysler Building, complete with gargoyle eagles.

Landmark:
The Morgan Library 33 East 36th Street. J. P. Morgan's opulent Italian Renaissance pile, a monument to the hoarding instinct.

Times Square

Times Square's pleasure-palace incarnation began in the 1890s, as the theatres began to move uptown, followed by restaurants and, ultimately, by the *New York Times*, which contrived to have the intersection of Broadway and Seventh Avenue at 42nd Street named after it. With its battery of vast electric signs in the 1920s, this stretch of Broadway became the Great White Way; its downhill slide began when the movies pushed 'legit' theatre into the side streets and wiped out vaudeville and burlesque entirely. By the mid-1960s, the movies themselves were squelched by TV and the carnival of porn was on. The great picture houses now run bottom-drawer kung fu and horror shows and scuzzy sex tableaux; the sidewalks flow with hot and cold running vice. This is an area in which to avert the eyes, but you might want to add it to your collection of Manhattan experiences anyway.

Theater District

New York's Theater District is concentrated in the mid- and upper 40s, between Broadway and Eighth Avenue. Unless you're stagestruck, you probably won't want to spring for interior views, but do steal a glance at the Lyceum and Helen Hayes Theater facades, on 45th and 46th Streets.

Midtown

Midtown Manhattan seems to extend farther vertically than horizontally – looking up invites vertigo. Boundaries are nebulous: approximately First and Sixth Avenues, from the Library at 42nd Street to the Plaza at 59th. Flags fly on Fifth Avenue, cheerful crowds surge up, down and across it, and on sunny days it positively sparkles. At 51st Street, St Patrick's dove-grey granite spires set off the austere charcoal limestone slabs of Rockefeller Center, across the avenue; the Channel Gardens (separating the Maison Française and the British Empire Building) and the golden Prometheus lead the eye upward to the RCA Building, a pearl among skyscrapers. Wander the labyrinth below Rockefeller Center: concourses of shops and restaurants, subterranean black marble elegance. Scope out the windows at Saks, Bonwit's, Bergdorf's.

Walk east to Madison. In the shadow of Grand Central, it's subdued and cavernous – the great conservative men's shops are clustered here. From here to 57th Street, the skyscrapers vie for light and air: advertising country. A block east, Park Avenue arrives at the pinnacle of wealth and urbanity. The Waldorf, St Bartholomew's, the beautiful bronze monolith of the Seagram Building, dominate the stage.

North of 59th Street, on Lexington, lies Dry Dock Country – named after a bank, and featuring Bloomingdale's: trendy (some say tacky) shopping for the parvenu. East, at the river's edge, lie Sutton Place and Auntie Mame's Beekman Place – the too-quiet bastions of the unbelievably rich; and the slab-and-mushroom headquarters of the UN, south of 48th Street.

Landmarks:

The New York Public Library: 41st Street and Fifth Avenue. Grand white marble, sublime inside and out. Guarded by the 'Library Lions', tranquil stone bookends.

Grand Central Terminal: 42nd Street and Park Avenue. The vast, vaulted interior, with its delicate pale-blue ceiling (complete with Zodiac), is unmatched for airiness and play of light.

Daily News Building: 220 East 42nd Street (between Second and Third Avenues). The peak of 1920s deco ornament. In the lobby, an immense revolving globe.

Upper East Side

The Upper East Side, from 59th Street to the 90s, between Third Avenue and Central Park, is high rent, high fashion, high hat. Madison becomes progressively more brilliant and expensive as you head uptown: the galleries classier, the boutiques more elegant, the prices more ludicrous. The broad upper reaches of Park Avenue are about evenly divided between the couches of absurdly rich psychiatrists and the aeries of the more-than-well-to-do, and the interstitial streets are filled with exquisite Beaux Arts townhouses. The mansions of bygone tycoons are mostly on Fifth Avenue, facing the park: the Frick Collection at 70th Street, the Commonwealth Fund at 75th, the NYU Institute of Fine Arts at 78th, the Marymount School at 84th, the Cooper-Hewitt Museum at 91st . . . these and scores of other semi-public palaces started life as pieds-à-terre for the coach-and-six trade. You'll need a good excuse to get into most of them. One place you have no excuse *not* to visit is the Metropolitan Museum, on the edge of Central Park, at 86th Street.

Landmarks:
Seventh Regiment Armory: 66th Street and Park Avenue. A vast brick fortress which manages not to look too out of place in these civilian climes.

The Whitney Museum: 75th Street and Madison Avenue. Another fortress: grey, forbidding granite cantilevered out above the entrance, with an asymmetrical cyclopean window.

Yorkville

Yorkville, the ancient Hungarian-German-Czech district just next door, runs from Third Avenue and the East River, between about 79th and 96th Streets, becoming progressively more run down as it moves north and east . . . but still a pleasant walk, especially if you're in search of food with a Central European accent. The quarter's only landmark is **Gracie Mansion**, the Mayor's residence in Carl Schurz Park, 88th Street, near the river: a graceful Colonial country house, perfectly incongruous in New York.

Upper West Side

The Upper West Side begins at Columbus Circle, the southwest corner of Central Park. **Lincoln Center**, a few steps north and west, caters to the concert trade: the New York Philharmonic, the Metropolitan Opera, the Juilliard School and other biggies draw immense crowds almost every night. The Gothic palazzos of Riverside Drive and the soaring apartment buildings of Central Park West have never lost the Midas touch. But from Columbus Avenue to West End, the 70s to the upper 90s were for forty years a dismal, battered slum; they're now enjoying – or suffering – a cataclysm of instant fashion. At the moment, the neighbourhood is half Spanish-speaking holdouts, half up-and-coming urban professionals with a serious case of Porsche-envy. Broadway, Amsterdam and Columbus are thronged with shoppers and strollers. Alongside the leftover *bodegas*, the delectable clothes, the fashionable food, you'll come across the monuments of New York's other heydays: the Ansonia, at 73rd Street and Broadway, where Caruso sang from the balconies; the Dakota, Central Park West and 73rd Street, a prestige address since the 1880s; the Cliff Dwellers' Apartments, 96th Street and Riverside Drive, with its curious Mayan-Deco facade. The New York Historical Society and the Museum of Natural History lie end-to-end along the Park at 77th Street, and if limitless collections captivate you, neither is to be missed.

The Heights and the Harlems

The Heights (Morningside, Hamilton, Washington) and the Harlems (Black and Spanish) take up the north end of the island. The Heights are given over to universities (Columbia, Barnard, Teachers College, the City College of New York), seminaries (Yeshiva, Union Theological Seminary), and the vast, unfinished pile of the Cathedral of St John the Divine, at 110th Street and Amsterdam Avenue. The 'ribbon' parks – Morningside, St Nicholas, Colonial – are *unsafe*: stay out of them. West, among the depressed and downtrodden streets of Harlem, there are pockets of great charm and elegance, the results of pre-ghetto land speculation and of careful maintenance over the years: the streets surrounding Mount Morris Park, the row houses and apartment buildings of

Sugar Hill along Eighth and Edgecombe Avenues, from 136th Street to the Morris-Jumel Mansion at 160th Street, and Striver's Row, the blocks between Seventh and Eighth Avenues at 138th and 139th Streets. Gentrification is in the wings. The ragged lower edges of Harlem – the blocks immediately above 110th Street – are the seediest and least safe, and here you should walk warily, and in company, if at all. Eastward, from Park Avenue to the river, lies Spanish (formerly Italian) Harlem – *El Barrio* – which had no patrician heritage to bequeath its inhabitants. In the shadow of the elevated tracks on Park Avenue, from 111th to 116th Streets, the outdoor *Marqueta* flourishes – everything from rosaries to tropical fruit – a lively summer morning's outing. But again, it's not an area in which to be too obviously a sightseer.

Rest stops

In addition to its parks, the city offers *plazas, atriums* and *lobbies* for the relief of weary pedestrians.

New York's **plazas** – the open spaces at the feet of skyscrapers – are a lavish gesture, installed by tycoons to impress other tycoons – corporate throwaway space. Fortunately for the populus, they almost always have convenient steps or waist-high walls on which to sit and chat, or have lunch, or watch traffic, or stare into the middle distance. A few:

A.T. & T. Building
Madison Avenue (between 55th and 56th Streets)
Alias the Phone Company – Philip Johnson's Chippendale chest-of-drawers. At the base, under the massive arches, there's a nest of tables and chairs, open to the wind but protected from the rain. Slightly gloomy but good for a breather.

Seagram Building
Park Avenue (between 52nd and 53rd Streets)
A 100-foot setback makes this an ideal spot for loafing: it almost democratizes this high-stepping stretch of Park Avenue.

Lincoln Center for the Performing Arts
Columbus Avenue (between 63rd and 65th Streets)
The plaza at the entrance to the Met is always well stocked with idlers, as well as skaters, lunchers and strollers. A few steps north, for those who prefer still waters, there's a large square pool in front of the Vivian Beaumont Theater. And Damrosch Park, at the southwest corner of the complex, for those who can't abide plazas.

For prime outdoor seating, don't forget the **Library steps** (42nd Street and Fifth Avenue) and the steps of the **Metropolitan Museum** (Central Park at 82nd Street). You'll have plenty of company, and generally free entertainment as well.

Atriums are now the rage among corporate giants – it's getting to the point where you can't slap up an international headquarters anywhere above 42nd Street without glassing in half the downstairs and stocking the place with desiccated trees, modern art and patio furniture. Happy the pedestrian, who now has somewhere to plant shopping bags and umbrella, shed dripping raincoat, and recoup the rational faculties. Many of these sanctuaries house shops and galleries as well as cafés; some even have rest rooms. A sampling:

Chemical Bank Building
277 Park Avenue (at 53rd Street)
The first atrium on the scene, dripping with greenery: it's stocked by the New York Botanical Garden. A very pleasant place to cool your heels.

Philip Morris Company
42nd Street and Park Avenue
Contains a gallery excerpted from the Whitney Museum and an espresso bar: you can sit at tables or on couches, knock back little cups of coffee and contemplate Claes Oldenburg's giant icebag.

I.B.M. Building
540 Madison Avenue (between 56th and 57th Streets)
A pleasant green-and-grey environment, rather like a conservatory garden: bamboo and glass. A Gallery of Art and Science shares the space: the last time I dropped by, a northwest-coast Indian was hacking gargoyles out of a thirty-foot cedar log.

The Park Avenue Plaza
55 East 52nd Street
A bland, cream-coloured interior with a very stylish perpendicular waterfall along one side. Plenty of expensive seating in the central café, but benches on the outskirts for the merely footsore.

Trump Tower
725 Fifth Avenue (at 57th Street)
A pretentious pink marble confection, entirely given over to the overpriced and unnecessary, with one high interior wall dedicated to a waterfall. Exterior balconies on the fourth and fifth floors are open to the public (and the weather); otherwise you can mortgage your children's inheritance in one of the lower-level restaurants.

The grand hotels of New York soothe their clientele with sumptuous **lobbies**, and these are open to the public: if you don't look too obviously out of place, you can settle into an easy chair or couch and pretend to be waiting for an audience with one of Zanuck's heirs, just in from the coast. Ten or fifteen minutes is about the limit, but it's enough to revive the spirits and allows you to track the comings and goings of the rich and powerful. For example:

The Plaza
59th Street and Fifth Avenue
This was said to be Frank Lloyd Wright's favourite hotel, though judging from reports of the cuisine it's unlikely that he ever ate here. The filigreed elevator doors are worth more than a passing glance. Turn-of-the-century elegance, with plenty of Art Nouveau motifs to amuse the eye.

The Grand Hyatt
42nd Street (between Lexington and Park Avenues)
The old Commodore Hotel, revamped by I.M. Pei: a vast lobby, five stories high (a trademark of the Hyatt chain), shimmering with polished brass, chrome and marble. Too glittery for a snooze.

The Palace
Madison Avenue (between 50th and 51st Streets)
The old Villard Mansions, formerly Random House headquarters, a trio of Italianate brownstones snapped up, revamped and adulterated by New York's current clan of property tycoons. The lobby is spacious but sterile, and it's low on seating: a scattering of circular benches. But, in these lofty reaches of Madison Avenue, it's all you're likely to find.

Housing:
hotels and alternatives

The inescapable fact of life for paupers is that there is no such thing as a bargain in New York hotels. Given the scarcity of real estate and the abundance of greed, you'll have to do some fancy footwork to avoid getting taken. Breakfast at the coffee shop in the Sheridan Center Hotel, for example – an overripe pleasure dome for conventioneers on Seventh Avenue – will set you back $8.50 before tax for two eggs, a roll and coffee – and this in a city where everyone knows that breakfast shouldn't cost more than $1.95. There are no limits to what some hotels will inflict on visitors: most people seem to expect to be overcharged and almost welcome it – but that doesn't mean *you* have to get carried home on your shield.

Many hotels that are even marginally affordable by paupers are going to be more than a little run down. If you must have all or even a couple of the comforts of home, be assured that you'll pay handsomely for them. At the same time you'll find it hard to survive in the city without at least a modicum of comfort and peace to come back to in the evenings or for an afternoon nap. Where to draw the line depends on your own sensibilities. I'd say that about $40 a night is the bare minimum – and fancy quarters are low on my list of priorities. Anything less is tantamount to sleeping under the 59th Street Bridge.

The good news is that there are a number of hotels in New York which, while neither rock-bottom in price nor palatial in aspect, do at least provide value for money: security, location, amenities, pleasant service, cleanliness, and a modicum of comfort are the desiderata, and although there are bound to be some trade-offs among these qualities in anything but a luxury hotel, the following will house you fairly well without bending your pocketbook out of shape.

If you're flat broke or simply can't abide hotels, your best bet is to stay with friends. If you know *anyone* in New York, don't hesitate to ask if they can put you up on the couch. Repay your visit in kind – plenty of dinners out and house presents, and of course an open invitation to visit you . . . Failing that, you might try:

Alternatives: Apartment exchanges and bed-and-breakfast arrangements are novel (to New Yorkers) solutions to the perennial problem of housing travellers. If you're willing to experiment, these could be your best bet. Or you can try roughing it: youth hostels and the YMCA. See Alternatives at the end of this section, p.74.

What to expect

Rule-of-thumb: the closer to the Plaza (59th Street and Fifth Avenue), the pricier the hotel. The upper east 50s and 60s are crowded with extravagant places: the Pierre, the Sherry, the St Regis, the Waldorf . . . I've included two or three exceptions to the rule in the list – small hotels which somehow exist in the shadow of New York's grand dames without actually liquidating their guests' assets. The problem with staying in this district is that it seems to foster big spending: you'll find yourself blowing money on cabs and pricey lunches out of sheer emulation. And unless you bought your clothes in the rue de Rivoli, you'll feel underdressed.

Along Sixth and Seventh Avenues, in the 50s, you'll find a number of immense commercial hotels – the Sheraton, the Hilton and such – most of them too big, impersonal and overpriced for our consideration. A few of the older 'tourist', rather than 'business', hotels are listed here for those who like the bustle of this area. A word of advice about these and other hotels that cater to groups: be sure to book a room in an upper storey – above the tenth floor, say – because package tours and conventioneers tend to be lumped together in the lower floors. What you don't need is the Elks running through the halls in party hats.

West of Fifth Avenue, in the 40s and lower 50s, are the shabbier and cheaper places of the Broadway and lower Midtown area. Most have seen better days; a few have seen worse, and are on the upswing. Generally, you'll find worn carpets, tired furniture, small rooms, narrow corridors, slow lifts – not calculated to lift your spirits after a day of slogging through the streets – but cheap and central. It's for circumstances like these that New York abounds with florists. A few daisies or irises will restore your mettle. You should be able to cadge a vase from the desk clerk.

Below and east of Fifth Avenue are the shabbier–yet hotels of the east 20s. The streets have little intrinsic interest, but the prospects on the borders of this little hotel-ghetto are fascinating: Murray Hill to the north, Gramercy Park to the south – both areas of serene gentility – and the new vitality of Second and Third Avenues to the east.

You'll also find a few oddball hotels scattered in the Village and the Upper East and West Sides. These are mostly residential and shopping districts, quieter than midtown but within easy range of the bright lights. Again, it's a matter of trade-offs: price v. comfort v. location. Whichever of these you value most will determine where you stay in New York. See the end of this section (p.73) for listings of hotels by district and cost.

Discounts

It's now fairly common for New York hotels – especially the big ones that cater to the expense-account crowd, who all go back to Dallas and St Louis after lunch on Friday – to offer special weekend rates. These can be as much as 40 per cent off in some cases for Friday and Saturday night packages (which can involve meals, tours, entertainment and what-have-you).

The New York Convention and Visitors' Bureau publishes an excellent Tour Package Directory twice a year (Fall/Winter and Spring/Summer). It spells out details on hotel packages (which can be booked directly through hotels) and tour packages (through travel agents only): most of these include sightseeing trips, Broadway shows, perhaps a meal or admission to the Empire State Building observation deck – experiences which you should be able to ferret out for yourself without hiring a middleman. But the pamphlet is well worth having for its up-to-date information on hotel 'specials'. Available free from:

New York Convention & Visitors' Bureau
2 Columbus Circle
New York, NY 10019

Rules, Constants, and Cautions

Booking in advance

See **Preliminaries** p.18.

If you find yourself in a room that's less than adequate, you don't necessarily have to abandon ship: especially in older hotels, the quality of accommodations can vary significantly from room to room. It doesn't hurt to ask to see another room – larger, or quieter, or more recently overhauled.

Extras

Rollaway beds for children or other family members are usually available at a small surcharge, though in many cases children under about age 14 stay free. If you're travelling with young children, it's worth checking in advance.

Phone, TV, private bath and air conditioning are the norm in all but the cheapest hotels. If you make phone calls from your hotel room, don't be surprised to find a hefty surcharge added to your bill. It's not a universal practice, but worth checking into when you arrive if you plan to spend a substantial amount of time on the phone.

Tipping is expected for services rendered: tip the bellman on a per-bag basis, and if you use room service (an unthinkable extravagance for paupers), add 15 per cent for the waiter.

Checking out and paying up

Checkout time in most hotels is noon or 1.00 p.m.

Credit cards: American Express, VISA, Mastercard (Access) and Diners Club are common currency in almost all hotels. We've noted the exceptions below.

Hotel rates will change without warning. The rates listed below were accurate up to September 1985; beyond that, we were answered with a shrug. Some hotels have seasonal rate schedules, which peak in summer and dip in winter. And prices tend to increase rapidly and phenomenally in this city of perpetual change.

One more item of financial news that sometimes takes visitors to New York by surprise: all hotels add $8\frac{1}{4}$ per cent city sales tax (a sort of VAT), plus a $2.00 room occupancy tax, to their rates. They're not padding the bill, but obeying the law.

Hotel listings

Each hotel is listed with its address, approximate location, zip code (the American postcode), and local phone number (the common 'area code' for Manhattan is 212).

Credit card abbreviations: AE = American Express, CB = Carte Blanche, DC = Diners Club, MC = Mastercard (Access), V = VISA.

Barbizon Hotel

140 East 63rd Street (between Park and Lexington Avenues), NYC 10021
838–5700

A charming, expensive, friendly and elegant hotel – formerly for women only – in a sleekish neighbourhood on the edge of 'Drydock Country'. Standard rates are $115 for a single room ($85 for a 'petite' single), and $135 for a double; weekend package rates, Friday night through Sunday morning, are about $100 per night for a double.

Bedford Hotel

118 East 40th Street (between Park and Lexington Avenues), NYC 10016
697–4800

A nice red-brick hotel on a pleasant street a couple of blocks from Grand Central Station. Kitchenettes. Rates: Singles $99–$120, doubles and twins $110–$130. Special weekend rates (and midweek during July and August): $89 for a single room, $99 for a double.

Hotel Beverly

125 East 50th Street (at Lexington Avenue), NYC 10022
753–2700

A relatively small, moderately-priced hotel around the corner from the Waldorf. The proximity of New York's arch-hotel seems to make the Beverly extend itself. The lobby is beautifully panelled, the rooms are a reasonable size, considering the neighbourhood and the price (about 12 by 15 feet for a standard bedroom), and the staff are pleasant and helpful. Single occupancy runs from $89 to $109, doubles $99–$119. A 'junior suite' (a larger room equipped with kitchenette) goes for $109–$129, and there are one- and two-bedroom suites available. Special 'no frills' weekend and seven-day rates. AE, CB, DC, MC, V.

Century Paramount Hotel

235 West 46th Street (between Seventh and Eighth Avenues), NYC 10036
764–5500

A theatre-district hotel with an enormous lobby, 600 rooms and about as much character as an air terminal. One advantage: you can make reservations directly in London by calling 01–242 9964; and they accept Euro and Barclay Cards, as well as VISA and the rest. Rates are priced seasonally. Summer: Single $52–$67; Double $58–$73; Twin $60–$75.

Chelsea Hotel

222 West 23rd Street (between Seventh and Eighth Avenues), NYC 10011
243–3700

Extreme funk. Rates for a double are from $60 to $75, without kitchen (they also cater to long-range clients). Lobby full of Warholesque art and artefacts, odd bits of furniture, incandescent colour scheme, and a population which could only be at home in the lobby of the Chelsea. A pleasant-enough manager; a riotous, run-down street, but close enough to the restaurants and relative peace of the Chelsea district. If the history of the 1960s interests you, this is where Warhol filmed Chelsea Girls, and it has housed multitudes of rock groups on the lower rungs of stardom. Virgil Thompson, the composer, has lived here for years. AE, V, MC.

Hotel Deauville

103 East 29th Street (between Park and Lexington Avenues), NYC 10016
683–0990

Very down-at-heel but not unfriendly. A single room is $45, a double is $50, and they don't take credit cards. Minimal accommodations.

Hotel Edison

228 West 47th Street (between Broadway and Eighth Avenue),
NYC 10036
840–5000

A theatre-district hotel, mammoth and cheap. Big, crumbling deco lobby with a startling show-biz mural in the corridor that leads in from the 46th Street entrance. Rates: $50–$56 for a single, $60–$66 for a double. Family rooms (two double beds for three or four family members) $69–$75. A rollaway bed for a fifth person in a family room is $7.50.

Hotel Empire

1889 Broadway (at 63rd Street), NYC 10023
265–7400

A big commercial hotel – 500 rooms – just south of Lincoln Center. The neighbourhood bustles with concert-goers at night, but lacks charm in daylight, and the hotel itself shares a monolithic graceless-ness with its surroundings. But it's respectable and well run. The Empire welcomes families and groups, and gives discounts to students, faculty, government employees (presumably US government, but perhaps British civil servants haven't tried yet), and clergy. Rates for single occupany, $70–$95; doubles $85–$110; additional persons $15; family rooms (up to four people) $90–$110. AE, CB, DC, MC, V.

Hotel Esplanade

305 West End Avenue, NYC 10023
874–5000

A big old pile on West End Avenue, mostly residential, with tenants who seem to have lived here all their lives, and accommodation for a few transients. The night manager has a characteristic New York charm: a brief moment of suspicion (what brings you in off the street at this hour of the night?) and a subsequent outpouring of charm and humour. Doubles: $72 (without kitchen). The nearest subway and bus route are several blocks away. No credit cards.

Excelsior Hotel

45 West 81st Street, NYC 10024
362–9200

A slightly (some would say *quite*) run-down hotel directly across from the Museum of Natural History and half a block from Central Park: perfect location if you like the Upper West Side; not particularly cordial, but the rates make up for that. Singles $51–$61, doubles $61–$71. Two-room suites run from $87 to $101 and have kitchenettes. This is the kind of hotel that goes 'residential' overnight (the housing situation in New York being the mob-scene that it is), so don't be surprised if the Excelsior has vanished by the time you arrive. AE, MC, V.

Gorham Hotel

136 West 55th Street (between Sixth and Seventh Avenues), NYC 10019
245–1800

Small and central. Every room has a kitchenette, including utensils (rare elsewhere). Small, bright lobby. Half the rooms are 2-room suites, set up like apartments. Room service is limited to continental breakfast. The Gorham is across the street from the old City Center Theater – elaborate Arabian-nights mosaics and plenty of dance. A good block and a reasonably pleasant, old-fashioned hotel. Single rooms $70–$80, doubles $80–$95. Additional persons $10–$20. One night's deposit, refundable upon 7 days' written notice. AE, CB, DC, MC, V.

Gramercy Park Hotel

2 Lexington Avenue (at 21st Street) NYC 10010
475–4320

'Moderate' rates, but a less than pristine lobby and a sullen desk clerk: his greeting to us was 'Yes?' Once a showplace, like many other hotels in the area, its public spaces show deterioration and lack of care. Its best point is the tranquillity of its setting: a view of Gramercy Park and the genteel brownstones around the square. They're slowly redecorating all the rooms: if the first one you see isn't up to snuff, ask for another. Doubles from $85 to $95. AE, CB, DC, MC, V.

Henry Hudson Hotel

353 West 57th Street (between Eighth and Ninth Avenues),
NYC 10019
265–6100

A nice, basic hotel, located on the less-fancy edge of 57th Street at Ninth Avenue. The basement is loaded with extras: a pool and a sauna. Rates are $60 for a single room, $70 for a double.

Iroquois Hotel

49 West 44th Street (between Fifth and Sixth Avenues),
NYC 10036
840–3080

A small midtown hotel, twin to the famous Algonquin, shabby but not unpleasant. Single occupancy from $50 to $85, double $55–$95, and suites (bedroom, living room, some with kitchenettes) from $65 to $95. Suites can accommodate up to four people, at $5 extra per person. AE, DC, MC, V.

Mansfield Hotel

12 West 44th Street (between Fifth and Sixth Avenues),
NYC 10036
944–6050

Quite shabby, reasonably friendly, and very cheap for a midtown hotel. 200 rooms. A single room with adjacent (shared) bath runs from $34 to $40. Singles with bath: $44–$48; doubles and twins $48–$55; suites for three $60–$70; suites for four to six: $80–$90. AE, DC, MC, V.

Hotel Martha Washington

30 East 30th Street (between Fifth and Madison Avenues),
NYC 10016
689–1900

Women only, and very accommodating. A big, clean lobby with lots of sitting-room. There's even a do-it-yourself laundry. One of the few hotels we came across with shared bath options. Single with running water, $28; singles with WC, $32; singles with bath, $40; twin with running water, $42; twin with bath, $55. The twin rates are per person; there's an added charge for an extra person. The Martha Washington also has unbeatable weekly rates – but stays are two weeks minimum and four weeks maximum.

Middletown Harley Hotel

148 East 48th Street (at Lexington Avenue), NYC 10017
755–3000

This is a Helmsley hotel – owned by a family which seems to have bought Manhattan back from the Dutch, and it's hard not to be prejudiced against them – but it's very nice: perhaps a bit stuffy. The lobby is small and demure, with lots of grey marble. Not cheap – singles are $105–$115, doubles $115–$125 – but good Friday-to-Sunday rates: $78 (single or double). AE, CB, DC, MC, V.

Novotel

226 West 52nd Street (on Broadway), NYC 10019
315–0100

New, slick, and expensive. A brash departure from the norm: brick and glass motifs. A branch of the vast French chain, and included here only for rich, nostalgic continentals. Single accommodations $115–$150, double $125–$170; additional persons $20. AE, DC, V.

Palace International

429 Park Avenue South (at 30th Street), NYC 10016
532–4860

Owned and managed by Indian restaurateurs, and staffed with a good deal of charm by Indians, the PI is a completely remodelled hotel on a somewhat chaotic and noisy stretch of Park Avenue South. The lobby is in soothing shades of grey and the reception is refreshingly courteous. Rates are $60 for a single room, $75 for a double. AE, DC, MC, V.

The River Hotel

180 Christopher Street (at West Street), NYC 10014
206–1020

Serves the Christopher Street ghetto, i.e. the gay community, but not exclusively. Very pleasant – the pink-and-grey school of interior decoration. Everything elegant and carefully thought out, but maybe a little self-conscious: hundreds of amenities offered, down to a choice of hard or soft pillows. Overlooks the Hudson; a few blocks from any sign of life, but within a few minutes' pleasant walk of the heart of the Village. Singles $75–$120, doubles $90–$135. AE, CB, DC, MC, V.

Roger Williams Hotel

28 East 31st Street (at Madison Avenue), NYC 10016
684–7500

Small and ugly, but adequate, hotel at the cheap end of Murray Hill. Tiny lobby, dingy hallways . . . but the rooms have (unequipped) kitchenettes, and the price is right. Singles from $50, doubles and twins from $55. Weekly rates: $225 and upwards for a single, $250 and upwards for a double. AE, MC, V.

Royalton Hotel

44 West Street (between Fifth and Sixth Avenues), NYC 10036
730–1344

Not much of a hotel, but centrally located. The management is less than outgoing; the place has come down in the world. Moderate rates: single rooms range from $50 to $85, doubles from $60 to $120. It'll do if you can't find a room anywhere else in the neighbourhood. AE, MC, V.

Salisbury

123 West 57th Street (between Sixth and Seventh Avenues),
NYC 10019
246–1300 or 800–223–0680

Informal clientele – full of French and British tourists. Nice, small, panelled lobby, efficient and courteous staff – the only drawback is that it's on 57th Street, which is a bit chaotic. 320 rooms – a medium-sized hotel by New York standards. Singles are $73–$83, doubles and twins $83–$93. Special weekend rates – $58 single or double, $68 for a triple – Friday and Saturday. AE, CB, DC, MC, V.

Hotel San Carlos

150 East 50th Street (between Lexington and Third Avenues), NYC 10022
755–1800

An odd little Spanish-stucco-style hotel located in the middle of a good block on the East Side – the San Carlos would probably look more at home in Los Angeles. The rooms may be a little too hispanic and ornate, and the price is a bit steep, but it's a friendly and quiet hotel. Singles from $99–$120, doubles or twins $110–$130. Weekend rates are about $10 cheaper than weekdays. Most rooms with fully equipped kitchenettes. All major cards.

Hotel Seville

22 East 29th Street (at Madison Avenue), NYC 10016
532–4100

Closed for renovations, but plans to reopen in May, 1986. A modest hotel across the street from the Little Church around the Corner. Literate travellers will recognize this as the hotel where the Moscow gumshoe and his girlfriend stayed in *Gorky Park*. In 1985, single occupancy rates were $61–$85; double $76–$100; additional persons $15 each – but these will escalate with renovation. The 1985 rates included a standard breakfast in the Seville's restaurant. Special rates for students, faculty, and clergy, and three-night packages (weekdays and weekends) with breakfast thrown in.

Shelburne Murray Hill

303 Lexington Avenue (at 37th Street), NYC 10016
689–5200

A rather deluxe hotel, one of eight in the Manhattan East chain. Single rooms $105, doubles and twins $115. If you're still reading this paragraph, note that the Shelburne is small, beautifully (if ornately) decorated and located in the genteel purlieus of Murray Hill. And despite the high weekday price tag, they do have plenty of Friday-to-Sunday bargain rates: $60 for a studio (one or two persons), $80 for a suite (one-four persons). AE, CB, DC, MC, V.

Shoreham Hotel

33 West 55th Street (between Fifth and Sixth Avenues), ·
NYC 10019
247–6700

Tiny and elegant. Desk man less than effusive; well-kept lobby,
excellent block: the Shoreham is next door to La Caravelle, one of
the more outrageously expensive eateries in town. The decor is less
than ornate – a rarity. Single rooms are $62–$72, doubles $76–$86,
$10 for each additional guest. Special weekend rates. Minimum
deposit of $50 for reservations, refundable on 48 hours' notice before
arrival date. AE, CB, DC, MC, V.

Hotel Tudor

304 East 42nd Street (between First and Second Avenues),
NYC 10017
986–8800

One of New York's most peculiar hotel lobbies: a hodge podge of
art deco decor, appliquéd mirrors, a thirtyish mural, a green-tiled
entryway. Apart from these oddities, the Tudor is small and unpretentious. Located a few blocks from the East River, near the UN,
and along a corridor that is rapidly filling up with expensive office
buildings. Advantage: there are hundreds of restaurants and plenty
of liveliness on Second and Third Avenues. Tiny studio rooms and
the smallest showers ever – you're better off asking for a tub when
you reserve. 'Family' rooms: 2 single and one double bed, or 4
singles. Singles $70–$75, doubles $80, twins $90, triples $120, quads
$130. AE, DC, MC, V.

Hotel Wales

1295 Madison Avenue (between 92nd and 93rd Streets),
NYC 10028
876–6000

A matter-of-fact hotel on the edge of a very expensive neighbour-
hood. Rates: $50–$60 for a double; refurbished suites for $100 plus.
Weekend rates slightly lower. The Wales, once a lovely hotel, is
sadly run down. The location is ideal for access to the Metropolitan
Museum and the galleries and boutiques of the upper East Side.
The lobby doubles as the entrance to the East-Side branch of
Sarabeth's Kitchen – a charming spot for breakfast. AE, CB, DC,
MC, V.

Washington Square Hotel

103 Waverly Place (just east of Washington Square), NYC 10011
777–9515

Formerly the Hotel Earle; now more than a bit tawdry, but hard
to beat for price. Generally a student population; borders on Washington Square, hence a rowdy atmosphere, especially on weekend
nights. Rates: $35 for a single, $46 for a double; $50 for a triple;
$60 for a quad. MC, V.

Hotel Wellington

871 Seventh Avenue (at 55th Street), NYC 10019
247–3900

838 rooms: basic accommodation in midtown. Some rooms have
kitchenettes, none have utensils. Big, and not overly charmed to
meet you. Full of groups, and a bit too preoccupied to take much
notice of waifs and strays. Single rooms $58–$75, doubles $68–$85;
suites $110–$150; third person (in twin rooms only) $10 additional.
AE, CB, DC, MC, V.

Westpark Hotel

308 West 58th Street (between Eighth and Ninth Avenues),
NYC 10019
246–6440

This might just be a discovery. Apart from its unassuming location
(it's on Columbus Circle, just south of the Coliseum, New York's
enormous exposition centre), the Westpark seems to be just right:
small, recently remodelled, well mannered, very tastefully decorated, and inexpensive. Single rooms are $45–$55, doubles $55–$65,
twins $60–$75, and suites $85–$115. AE, MC, V.

Wyndham Hotel

42 West 58th Street (between Fifth and Sixth Avenues),
NYC 10019
753–3500

A well-polished gem in a pricey street. Not over-expensive (by New
York standards), it caters to the theatrical trade, and tries to keep
a low profile. Very punctilious reception. No room service. Book
well in advance. Single rooms $82–$90, doubles $92–$100. AE, CB,
DC, MC, V.

Comparative shopping:

Hotels listed from cheapest to priciest, based on minimum rates for a double room.

	Single rooms		Double rooms	
	Min.	Max.	Min.	Max.
	$	$	$	$
YMCA/William Sloan House	24	Alternatives, (see below)		
YMCA Vanderbilt Branch	24			
Hotel Martha Washington	28	40	42	55
Washington Square Hotel	35		46	
Mansfield	34	48	48	55
Hotel Wales		50	60	
Hotel Deauville	45		50	
Westpark Hotel	45	55	55	65
Iroquois Hotel	50	85	55	95
Roger Williams Hotel	50		55	
Century Paramount Hotel	52	67	58	73
Chelsea Hotel			60	75
Hotel Edison	50	56	60	66
Royalton Hotel			60	120
Excelsior Hotel	51	61	61	71
Hotel Wellington	58	75	68	85
Hotel Esplanade			72	
Palace International	60		75	
Henry Hudson	60		70	
Hotel Seville	61	85	76	111
Hotel Shoreham	62	72	76	86
Hotel Tudor	70	75	80	
Gorham Hotel	70	80	80	95
Salisbury	73	83	83	93
Hotel Empire	70	95	85	110
The River Hotel	75		90	
Wyndham Hotel	83	90	92	100
Gramercy Park Hotel	85	95	90	100

| | Single rooms | | Double rooms | |
	Min.	Max.	Min.	Max.
	$	$	$	$
Barbizon Hotel	85	115	135	165
Hotel Beverly	89	109	99	119
Bedford Hotel	99	120	110	130
Hotel San Carlos	99	120	110	130
Middletown Harley Hotel	105	115	115	125
Shelburne Murray Hill	105		115	
Novotel	115	150	125	170

Hotels listed by location:

Chelsea:

Chelsea Hotel
YMCA/William Sloan House

Gramercy:

Hotel Deauville
Gramcery Park Hotel
Hotel Martha Washington
Palace International
Roger Williams Hotel
Hotel Seville

Greenwich Village:

The River Hotel
Washington Square Hotel

Lincoln Center:

Hotel Empire

Midtown East:

Barbizon Hotel
Hotel Beverly
Middletown Harley Hotel
Hotel San Carlos
Hotel Tudor
YMCA Vanderbilt Branch

Midtown West:

Gorham Hotel
Henry Hudson
Iroquois Hotel
Mansfield Hotel

Midtown West (Continued)	Novotel
	Royalton Hotel
	Salisbury
	Hotel Shoreham
	Hotel Wellington
	Westpark Hotel
	Wyndham Hotel
Murray Hill:	Bedford Hotel
	Shelburne Murray Hill
Theater District:	Hotel Edison
	Century Paramount Hotel
Upper East Side:	Hotel Wales
Upper West Side:	Hotel Esplanade
	Excelsior Hotel

Alternatives
Exchanges

Some hints and possibilities:
1 Make your arrangements through an exchange agency. Two good ones are:
Worldwide Home Exchange Club
139a Sloane Street
London SW1
and
Intervac
6 Siddals Lane, Allestree
Derby DE3 2DY
Or check the Announcements column in *The Times*, London.

2 Be specific about what you're offering: number of bedrooms, baths, use of telephone and utilities, exact dates of departure and return. If pet- or plant-sitting is part of the deal, don't hold back the details.

3 Make sure you know what you're getting in exchange: not just the basics, but some idea of the neighbourhood (and if it's not in Manhattan, the nearest transport). If you have friends in New York, have them do a little discreet scouting.

4 Be prepared for a protracted transatlantic correspondence, and a hefty phone bill. Don't be too chagrined if everyone's plans change or fall apart in the middle of negotiations: be flexible, and be prepared to try again. And do keep in mind that if everything falls miraculously into place, exchanges are by far the most comfortable and least exorbitant solution to the housing crunch in New York.

Bed & breakfast

A number of New Yorkers have discovered that acting as B&B hosts is a perfectly healthy way to combat the exorbitant cost of living in the city: an occasional set of house guests supplements the rent and they may well turn out to be charming acquaintances. Visitors to the city can only benefit: the rates are relatively low, the surroundings are domestic, and the experience of New York is far more genuine than hotels can provide.

New York currently has four B&B options:

Urban Ventures

PO Box 426
New York, NY 10024
594–5650

Biggest and best organized of the bunch, UV has a line on hundreds of apartments in Manhattan (and some in Brooklyn and Queens): brownstones, lofts, penthouses, highrises and what-have-you. Continental breakfast is included in the deal. You choose the price range and the neighbourhood and they'll try to place you. With enough advance notice, you should get just what you want. It's a highly customized operation: Urban Ventures' brochure includes a detailed application form with such questions as Age group? Allergic to pets? Do you smoke? Need a crib?

Rooms with private baths run from $50 to $75 for a double, $38–$50 for a single; with shared bath, $32–$50 for a double, $23–$36 for a single. And entire apartments without hosts begin at $50 per night.

There's a minimum stay of two nights, $40 per person deposit in advance, with the balance paid on arrival, and a key deposit of $25, collected by your host and refunded on return of the keys.

New World Bed & Breakfast

150 Fifth Avenue, Suite 711
New York, NY 10011
675–5600

New World does most of its business by phone, but if you plan well ahead you should be able to negotiate by correspondence. If you do phone them, their office hours are 10.00 a.m. – 4.00 p.m. New York time (subtract five hours from Greenwich Mean Time). Terms are about the same as 'Urban Ventures': rates run from $28 to $65 for single occupancy, $40 to $75 double: most are in the $50–$60 range. No-host apartments run from $60 to $200. A 25 per cent deposit is required in US funds.

The B&B Group: New Yorkers at Home

301 East 60th Street
New York, NY 10022
838–7015 (9.00 a.m.–4.00 p.m., Monday through Friday)

I had a hard time getting past their busy signal, and the eventual voice on the other end was friendly but a bit harassed . . . which says something about the transient housing situation in New York. Their brochure looks as if it was slapped together while the proprietor was on the phone. Terms: $40–$55 for a single, $55–$70 for a double. International Money Orders are accepted in US funds only.

Hosts and Guests, Inc.

Box 6798, FDR Station
New York, NY 10150
874–4308 (9.00 a.m. – 11.00 a.m., 4.00 p.m. – 7.00 p.m., Monday through Saturday)

A bit flaky on the phone, but cordial. Their basic terms are about as those listed above – their brochure is somewhat sketchy. Rates: $40–$50 for single occupancy, $50–$65 double.

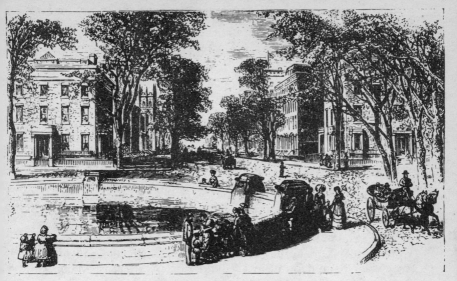

WASHINGTON SQUARE AND FIFTH AVENUE.

Student Housing, Youth Hostels and the 'Y'

International House of New York

500 Riverside Drive (at 123rd Street), NYC 10027
678–5036

In the Columbia University neighbourhood, for students only, on a semester basis, in dormitories. Singles about $25; $48 for three nights.

International Student Center

38 West 88th Street, NYC 10024
787–7706

Dorm space – six to ten people per room – for about $6, but only for people under 30, with foreign passports. Five days maximum stay.

Student Hospice

154 East 33rd Street (between Lexington and Third Avenues),
NYC 10016
228–7470

Dorm space at about $18; private rooms for $25. Students only,
with a one-week limit.

YMCA Vanderbilt Branch

224 East 47th Street (between Second and Third Avenues),
NYC 10017
755–2410

Single rooms $24–$34. Twin (bunk beds) for two people $16 per
person. Triple $15. Quad $14. Bedrooms are private, with colour
TV; bathrooms are at the end of each corridor. No personal cheques
(except for room deposit, in US funds) or credit cards. Maximum
stay 25 days. There are some rather odd people running around
the 'Y' and it's anything but luxurious – but the price is unbeatable,
and the location is excellent. And it's 'co-ed'.

City cuisine

Apartment life in New York has at least two things in common with beehives, anthills, termite nests and other natural habitats: the absence of elbow-room and the presence of insects. Nobody can do anything about the second of these, but there's a perfect solution to the first: restaurants. When New Yorkers need a place to spread out, to unwind with friends or work out business deals, to command an audience or cosy-up to other New Yorkers, they seek out new places to eat. Entire strata of city society define themselves by where and what they eat, and fashions in food change as rapidly and arbitrarily as hemlines. A selection of possibilities follows, from stand-up pizza-by-the slice to Argentinian *tapas*, none of it so expensive (or so cheap) as to deprive you of your appetite, and all of it served in establishments where the company is at least as interesting as the food.

There are plenty of occasions when it's perfectly okay not to order a full meal: if the restaurant isn't wildly busy you can get along on a series of appetizers without offending the staff, or split entrées (or dessert or salad) with a companion: helpings are large. And if you're in no hurry and feel adventurous, you can eat each course in a different place.

A pauper's approach to food in New York needs a delicate combination of wariness and adventure: an ability to avoid being suckered into exorbitant checks for mediocre food; a talent for spotting regional and ethnic specialities on the cheap.

One strategy that works well is to take advantage of the city's ubiquitously cheap breakfast rates: find a congenial nearby coffee shop (for some reason New York's Greek population holds the monopoly on these) and load up on eggs, toast, 'hash-brown' potatoes (with onions, for some Mediterranean reason) and coffee. $1.40 plus a thirty-cent tip should see you through; another thirty cents will get you the *Times*. Stay *out* of hotel coffee shops, which specialize in robbing tourists.

Lunch can be a hand-held affair in the streets, or taken seated in a vest-pocket park or plaza: you can pick up all sorts of exotica from sidewalk vendors and hole-in-the-wall pizza merchants; you can venture among the take-out salad bars (Korean monopoly) along the busier boulevards and pick up sliced fruit or steamed vegetables; or you can take a full-blown restaurant lunch and skimp on dinner.

Prices listed are before drink, tax and tip, and *they will change* almost before your eyes.

For convenience, restaurants are listed here by neighbourhood. See Getting Around Town, p.31, if you're not yet familiar with the territory.

Chelsea
Blue Plate

150 Eighth Avenue (between 17th and 18th Streets)
255–8516

Pasta, chilli, sandwiches, and salads, cheap and plain, served cafeteria-style with a maximum price-tag of $4.00. The decor is minimal – but includes a healthy dose of turquoise vinyl.

Cajun

129 Eighth Avenue (at 16th Street)

Bayou specialities, which these days are so popular that they're getting on everyone's nerves. Spicy baked whole crabs are $4.95; blackened bluefish (sautéed very fast with about a quarter-inch of garlic and red pepper embedded in the skin) is $9.95; jambalaya (rice, pork, smoked sausage, ham) is $5.95; and a shrimp-and-crab gumbo (the active ingredient is okra) is $6.50.

Chelsea Foods

198 Eighth Avenue (between 19th and 20th Streets)
691–3948

A pleasant place for lunch, though a trifle cramped. The restaurant area is tucked behind a compact delicatessen – of the 'gourmet' variety, as opposed to the Kosher extravaganza. Specialities are pasta, chicken and veal entrées for dinner (from $6.00 to $10.00); sandwiches and salads – including a very good cold pasta salad – for lunch, from $4.00 to $6.00.

Empire Diner

210 Tenth Avenue (corner of 22nd Street)
243–2736

The first 'converted' diner: a giant step up from its former greasy-spoon incarnation; now chic and glittery (the Manhattan term is 'glitzy') and a visual if not a culinary delight. Open all night.

Quatorze

240 West 14th Street (between Seventh and Eighth Avenues)
206–7006

This place was recommended by a friend as 'Cator's' and I had a hell of a time finding it. Too elegant (and with too high-stepping a clientele) for the general dereliction of West 14th Street. Beautifully designed, with a marble bar, black-and-white tile floor, and magnificent French posters, and correspondingly priced: a terrine or *jambon persillé* is $4.25; duck with green peppercorn sauce is $13.50; grilled flounder with meunière sauce is $13.95. Open for lunch Monday-Friday, and seven days from 6:00 to midnight. AE only.

Rogers & Barbero

149 Eighth Avenue (between 17th and 18th Streets).
243–2020

Wood and marble interior, elegant and comfortable. Entrées in the $8.00 range for lunch: sole with herbs, shrimp in a white wine sauce, veal and wild rice salad.

Whole Grain

7 West 19th Street
206–7518

On a street full of photographers' lofts – consequently, Whole Grain is full of models and other healthy, well-dressed people. The room is simple and elegant, and the food is good if you go in for macro-biotics: rice, lentils, vegetables, sprouts, tofu and other soy by-products, all scrambled together. About $8.00 for lunch.

East Village
Cloister Cafe

238 East 9th Street (between Second and Third Avenues)
777–9128

A lovely place in an unlikely location, for espresso and sandwiches. The room is long and dark, with stained glass windows filtering the light at one end – a chapel-like effect. The side door lets on to a shady, cobblestoned terrace, with a fountain trickling into a long, narrow pool, and if you find yourself in the East Village on a hot day it's a perfect spot to regain your senses. Light food: salads and omelettes, bagels, lox and cream cheese, in the $5.00 range. No credit cards.

Evelyne's

87 East 4th Street (between Second Avenue and the Bowery)
254–2550

Dinner for the off-off-Broadway crowd, i.e. recherché glitz. A warmly lit, pleasant interior, with a bar in front, and generally an excellent gallery of pictures on the walls. The crowd is showy and the atmosphere is unlikely to be intimate. Fricasee of chicken with ham and oysters: $10.50; pompano in beurre noire with pickled peppers: $14.75. You get the idea. My one shot here was rabbit in a syrupy prune sauce, delicious and weird. Open Monday-Saturday for dinner. AE only.

Odessa

117 Avenue A (between 7th and 8th Streets)
473–8916

Russian, cheap, filling, and age-old. Clientele: quasi-punk Lower East Side youth and the last remnants of New York's Russian community. For $4.00 you can have a meal of salad, bread, entrée, vegetable, and potatoes. Five different specials daily. Best known for piroshskis and kilbasa, and their blintzes are not bad at all. Breakfast served till midnight (this appeals to Americans, somehow) for $1.25. Odessa spends its off hours as a coffee shop, hence short on atmosphere, but a maximum price tag of $6.00 offsets this.

Phebe's

361 Bowery (at East 4th Street)
473–9008

Sandwiches, omelettes, burgers, and such in the neighbourhood of $3.00 to $5.00. A large, fresh, delicious spinach salad with big crumbs of bacon was $4.25; it took about twenty minutes to arrive, but no one's in a rush in these parts. Phebe's looks out on the parade at the top end of the Bowery, which ranges from punk to drunk – the upwardly mobile end of the street. A young crowd inside, easy atmosphere, eclectic juke box, and surprisingly good coffee.

Second Avenue Kosher Delicatessen

10th Street and Second Avenue

Straightforward New York food: pastrami, boiled beef flanken, potato knishes, noodle pudding, gefilte fish.

Ukrainian Restaurant & Caterers

132 Second Avenue (at 11th Street)
533–6765

Recently reopened after a move, with outdoor seating in the summer, but otherwise changeless: the local Russian-speaking population wouldn't stand for it. Best bet is a combination platter for $6.95: stuffed cabbage, four kinds of piroshki (filled dumplings, known here as pierogi), bigos (sausage, cabbage and beef), kilbasa (Polish sausage), bread and salad. Beet borscht is $1.50 per cup, and flaczk (tripe soup!) $2.25. And you can have potato pancakes with sour cream or apple sauce for $4.25.

Garment District
Gefen's

297 Seventh Avenue (at 27th Street)
929–6476

A Kosher vegetarian dairy restaurant, with waiters and clients in hats and yarmulkes: evidence of orthodoxy. Plain Jewish cooking: blintzes (potato, cheese, kasha, jelly, $5.25); kreplachs (the Jewish equivalent of ravioli) and potato pancakes, matzo brei, gefilte fish, whitefish or carp, baked or broiled, sandwiches and specials: a good simple goulash with stuffed cabbage for about $6.00.

Hershey Dairy Restaurant

167 West 29th Street (between Seventh and Eighth Avenues)
868–6988

A kosher dairy restaurant along the same lines as Gefen's, above, but smaller and clubbier: Hershey's caters to the wholesale furriers who line both sides of 29th Street.

Gramercy
Madras Palace

104 Lexington Avenue (between 27th and 28th Streets)
684–0565

Vegetarian cuisine from South India: not so wickedly spiced as the North Indian and Pakistani varieties, and heavier on the legumes, but quite delicious. Dinner about $9.00 if you stay away from expensive side-orders.

Pete's Tavern

129 East 18th Street (at Irving Place)
473–7676

An old-fashioned saloon interior, with a casual restaurant tucked away behind it. Great hamburgers, and not bad pasta dishes. For about $8.00 I had excellent mussels in a hot tomato sauce with good bread to soak it up with, and a side order of spaghetti. The lunch crowd (and it is crowded) is well-dressed and business-like, the service fast, efficient and friendly.

Shaheen Sweet's

99 Lexington Avenue (at 27th Street)

A limited but delicious menu of curries and birianis, and an outrageous supply of super-sweet Indian oddments: jelabies – deep-fried twists of lentil batter, soaked in syrup; peda and burfy – milk (technically buffalo milk) reduced and sugared to its fudge-like essence; batisa – layered, flaky chick pea flour, sugar, nuts – all under $1.00. A *thalee* or platter of chicken, mutton, or vegetable curry, with nain or chapattee, raeeta or salad, is served cafeteria style, comes to $5.00, and is served on paper plates and styro containers – but you're not here for gracious living. Bring your own beer if you like.

Lower East Side
Seaport Food Hall

19 Fulton Street (in the South Street Seaport,
between Fulton and John Streets at the East River)
608–0642

This is New York's version of the Covent Garden renovation: the former Fulton Fish Market has been banished to Brooklyn and replaced with a collection of snack bars and restaurants. More stalls than the Kentucky Derby. Chinese steamed rolls, French pastry, German sausages, Greek souvlaki, Indian tikka, Italian pasta, Japanese sushi, and Mexican tacos; stands dedicated to burgers, clams, cookies, eggs and egg creams, empanadas, fried chicken, fudge, jellybeans, nuts, onion rings, pastrami, and yogurt. A reckless person could get very sick here. If the second-floor food hall fails to satisfy, there are restaurants scattered among the floors below, including an oyster bar.

Midtown

Automat

200 East 42nd Street (at Third Avenue)
599–1665

The final automat: a dazzling concept at mid-century, now fizzled. A solid wall of glassed-in pigeonholes, each with a sandwich or a piece of pie and a coin-slot which pops the door open. Beautiful nickel-plated spigots dispense coffee and tea. The clientele was never New York's glossiest, but the food has always been abundant, good and cheap. There's a steam table at one end of the room where you can still get hot cereal – a vanishing species – for breakfast, and other fairly basic food at all times.

Bienvenue

21 East 36th Street, (off Madison Avenue)
684–0215

Tiny tables in the French style, in two half-panelled/rough-plastered rooms, and a large business crowd at lunch, relatively well behaved for New Yorkers. Moules ravigote, minced and smothered in a capery tartare sauce, were $2.50; an enormous quiche, perfect, rich, and easily enough for two, was $6.50. And the service is fast, the atmosphere unpressured and comfortable.

Carnegie Delicatessen

854 Seventh Avenue (between 54th and 55th Streets)
727–2245

Classic 'Broadway' deli; not cheap but high quality, and indomitable waiters. Elbow-to-elbow. Huge sandwiches with cutesy names: 'The Egg and Oy', 'Nova on Sunday'. Cold borscht, lox and bagels, cheesecake, tourists.

Costello's

225 East 44th Street (between Second and Third Avenues)
599–9614

A hangout for *Daily News* reporters: bar up front, tables in two partitioned rooms behind. The bar is cluttered with musty trophies and sports paraphernalia, and the language is ripe. The left-hand dining room has original Thurber drawings etched into the walls – a kind of crude fresco – transported bodily from Costello's previous location. The waiters are dog-eared, the service slow but kindly, and the menu is German-Irish, in the $7 range.

Darbar

44 West 56th (between Fifth and Sixth Avenues)
432–7227

For $9.95, an all-you-can-eat Indian buffet lunch. Indian breads, chicken tikka, several curries, assorted condiments and chutneys, pilaus: an amazing assortment. The restaurant is elegant and caters to the suit-and-tie trade (and the few open-collared types who've discovered the buffet). The dining room is upstairs, above the bar, and the service is instant and friendly.

Oyster Bar

Grand Central Terminal, lower level
490–6650

Moderately expensive, busy, and big: a wonderful tiled, cavernous room. Oysters of all varieties: you can buy them singly for $1.50 (!) or by the half-dozen, on the half-shell. Every possible species of fish, simply cooked, in the $7.00–$22.00 range. They serve delicious crumbly 'bisquits' with everything. Closed Saturday and Sunday. AE, CB, DC, MC, V.

Pax Cafe

205 West 57th Street (between Seventh and Eighth Avenues)
956–3726

For a simple, filling lunch in clean, well-ordered surroundings. Besides the normal spread of sandwiches, salads and omelettes, they serve a variety of pastas, from crabmeat pasta to spinach tortellini, and everything seems to come in 'large' or 'medium' portions. Prices range from $4.00 to $10.00, averaging around $6.00.

Stage Delicatessen

834 Seventh Avenue (between 53rd and 54th Streets)
245–7850

Another 'classic' deli: good food, great waiters and waitresses, somewhat touristy clientele, and semi-high prices. Kasha varniskas (kasha with pasta, onions, mushrooms, brown sauce). Hot or cold borscht with sour cream. Sandwiches named after showbiz celebs.

Murray Hill
Balkan Armenian

129 East 27th Street (between Lexington and Park Avenues)
689–7925

Armenian cooking – to my mind surpassing its Greek, Syrian, Lebanese relatives – has a kind of gentle good nature to it, well worth seeking out. The Balkan is one of the few remaining Armenian holdouts in New York (and you'll find some of the city's few remaining Armenians eating there). Appetizers – hommos, tarama, and unbelievably tender stuffed vine leaves – are about $4.00; entrées (most having to do with lamb, rice pilaff, currants and pine nuts) are about $10.00. A thin, crackly unleavened bread starts things off and sweet, muddy Armenian coffee ends them.

Chiaki

396 Third Avenue (between 28th and 29th Streets)
696–4920

High decibel hip Japanese. Excellent sushi (which seems to vary little in price or quality in New York), outsize clothes, slick neon decor, and a killer juke box. A fairly staid assortment of sushi (tuna, shrimp, etc.) was $11.95; ordering à la carte increases both the range and the possibility of dropping your life savings on raw fish.

Sarge's Delicatessen

548 Third Avenue (between 36th and 37th Streets)

Sarge's is big, bright, and brassy. Plenty of food, plenty of loud chatter, and a fair amount of friendly banter. I can't think of a better place for a pastrami-on-rye when the mood strikes. Next door they've opened a sort of gourmet pastry deli, which I stay out of on principle. Open 24 hours, seven days a week.

SoHo
Fanelli

94 Prince Street (at Mercer Street)
226–9412

A cheap (for SoHo) and lively corner cafe: pasta, quiche, shepherd's pie, mussels, and heros in the $6.00 range. Tile floor, checked tablecloths, no credit cards. Open seven days till 2:00 a.m.

Theater District
The three Market Diners: West 43rd at Eleventh Avenue/ West 33rd at Ninth Avenue/West and Laight Street

All-night, full of stainless steel, with wrap-around parking lots. Cabbies, cops, punks, and slumming elegantsia. Specials: meatballs and spaghetti ($4.30), pot roast and potato pancakes ($6.50). Highway cuisine. Minimum check: 50 cents per customer. Thick coffee.

TriBeCa
El Internacional

219 West Broadway (at White Street)
226–8131

Best for *tapas* – hot Castillian hors d'oeuvres – which you can order in the bar while you peruse the crowd. The garish glass-and-tile interior was inherited from a previous incarnation as a Mafia dive; it's now swarming with charming, inept waiters. Delightful and (in 1985, anyway) a recent discovery, hence 'in', but, with luck, by the time you read this it will no longer be fashionable. *Tapas* come in all flavours: champignons al Jerez, berenharas morunas (Moroccan-style eggplant), gambas al ajillas (shrimp in garlic sauce), ceviche (marinated raw scallops), calamaras a la plancha (grilled squid), and so on ad infinitum. Prices are about $2.50–$4.00 for a mouthful, $4.50 to $8.50 for a small serving: the Castillian equivalent of sushi.

Laughing Mountain Bar & Grill

148 Chambers Street (off West Broadway)
233–4434

Slick and cute. Since it's only on the fringe of TriBeCa, it's not blatantly overpriced. An oddball menu: for appetizers, black bean soup ($2.75) and cold Szechuan noodles (with the ubiquitous and addictive red-pepper-and-peanut-butter sauce – $3.50); a zucchini fritata with basil and parmesan is $5.50; a curried chicken salad is $7.00. For a less trendy menu, duck into Hamburger Harry's, diagonally across Chambers Street, for burgers of every stripe, all charcoal broiled, under $5.00.

Riverrun

176 Franklin Street (off Hudson Street)
966–3894

Small, with a lively bar in front and seafood and such behind: decorated with watercolours and photography. Daily specials in chalk at the front window: I had chicken persillé for $7.95, moderately good, at a very moderate price for this part of town. Seafood entrées include a striped bass bouillabaisse, broiled bay scallops, and smoked trout, from $7.95 to $9.75.

Upper East Side
1st Wok

1570 Third Avenue (at 88th Street)
410–7747

A mini-chain of Szechuan Chinese fast-food restaurants. Lunch is cheap and delicious: $3.75 for Szechuan standards, such as chicken and broccoli, shrimp, bean curd Szechuan-style, etc. Tea and rice included. A tiny room made larger by a mirrored wall; quick and not-too-personal service; small tables and little elbow-room but overall an excellent place for a quick bite. Bar service, too. Identical branches at 1384 First Avenue (74th Street), 582 Second Avenue (between 33rd and 34th Streets), and 1374 Third Avenue (between 78th and 79th Streets).

7th Regiment Armory Mess

643 Park Avenue (between 66th and 67th Streets, 4th floor)
288–0200 (National Guard recruiting office)

Dinner only, 5.00–9.00 p.m.

Included here as a curiosity. Greetings at the entrance from an M.P.; directions to the 4th-floor Mess via elevator. Down a wide, panelled corridor, through faded red curtains and a bar, into an immense 'half-timbered' dining hall, with tables scattered about and a fireplace at one end. White tablecloths laid over blue ones; heavy nickel flatware; butter squares on ice; salt rolls. The waitresses call you 'Hon' (short for 'Honey'). Black bean soup or consommé; shrimp cocktail; shell steak, lamb chops, pork chops; ice cream or rice pudding. American food at its most basic. Entrées range in price from about $7.00 to $12.00.

The New Amity

1134 Madison Avenue (between 84th and 85th Streets)
861–3255

This little place serves the best cornmeal muffins I ever tasted. Otherwise it's standard coffee-shop fare: hamburgers, salads, sandwiches. Good for a mid-morning or afternoon snack if you're in the neighbourhood of the Metropolitan Museum. One wall is covered with an immense impasto rendering of sailboats in Long Island Sound, which will either soothe your eyes on a cold winter day or put you off your food.

Zucchini

1336 First Avenue (between 71st and 72nd Streets)
249–0559

An amiable vegetarian/seafood restaurant with the added attraction of delicious food. It's full of plants, flowers, and antique wood; the service is quick and friendly, and the only items on the menu that don't quicken the pulse are 'vegetarian burgers'. Otherwise: a list of five pastas with five sauces (including a very macho aiolli, which caused heads to turn) – $5.95; sandwiches, quiches, salads; and specials – shrimp primavera, e.g. – with steamed vegetables and brown rice, $12.95.

Upper West Side
Forest & Sea International

477 Amsterdam Avenue (at 83rd Street)
580–7873

Thai/French food in a large, panelled, partitioned room. It's locally known as 'Fur and Feather'. When I first walked in, this place was in the throes of discovery: a chic crowd fawning over harried waitresses. Within three months it had opened a branch on

Broadway. Ginger rabbit, in a light soy sauce with ginger and mushrooms, is $7.25, simple and delicious; côte du porc with onions and hoisin sauce, $7.25. The crowd is Upper West Side but not obnoxiously trendy.

Genoa

271 Amsterdam Avenue (between 73rd and 74th Streets)
797–1094

Small and busy: they don't take reservations, and before each of two dinners here I had to stand in line in the doorway at least fifteen minutes. The rewards were prodigious: scallopine in a Marsala sauce which I almost swooned into. The runner-up was again scallopine, this time with a lemon-and-white wine sauce. Both about $8.00. Excellent pasta in perfect marinara sauce. Fast, overworked service: the place seems to be run entirely by two waiters and a cook. Included here at the risk of increasing the queue to half an hour.

Indian Oven

285 Columbus Avenue (between 72nd and 73rd Streets)
362–7567

Northern Indian cuisine served upstairs and downstairs. The speciality is Tandoori chicken, marinated in yoghurt and spices and baked. Kormas, masalas, vindaloos, birianis in the $8.00–$10.00 range.

Kikusushi Dosanko and Dosanko Larmen

2025 Broadway (between 69th and 70th Streets)
496–0074

A pair of Japanese fast-food restaurants, with branches elsewhere around town. The sushi and sashimi are in the $0.80–$2.00 range, which is low for these addictive little items. Larmen is the Japanese version of Chinese lo mein – soft noodles. The Dosanko joints are short on atmosphere, limited in scope, but low-budget. The basic larmen are served hot with simple sauces: soy sauce, bean paste, salted butter, curry, and with or without strips of beef or pork. If you like your noodles *al dente*, the word is *oishii*. Fast and filling, and less than $5.00.

Popover Cafe

551 Amsterdam Ave (between 86th and 87th Streets)
595–8555

A tiny square room with high ceilings, specializing in popovers: delicate little blimps of unsweetened pastry, fresh out of the oven, served with butter (plain or flavoured) and preserves. These are served singly or in baskets of three and, depending on quantity and accompaniments, the prices range from 75 cents to $1.00 each. Popovers are a quintessentially American experience, like patchwork quilts and Grandma Moses, and this is an excellent place to find them. The P.C. also serves rather eccentric sandwiches in the $5.00–$6.00 range (Black Forest ham, chicken, Gruyère, bacon, tomato and Russian dressing – that's one sandwich, not six), omelettes, soups, salads, suicidal desserts and exotic coffees and teas. The service is pleasant but a little scatterbrained, and the place occasionally has patrons lined up outside. Breakfast on weekends at 10.00 a.m.; closing at 11.00 p.m. six days a week, 9.00 p.m. on Sundays. No credit cards.

Song Thai

2286 Broadway (between 82nd and 83rd Streets)
799–0073

A curious interior – fabric behind light wood frames, small gilt figures, odd potted palms. Taped Thai violin melodies, reminiscent of Irish folk songs. Appetizers: spring rolls or khanom jeep: steamed dumplings, hot but delicate, with two sauces, $4.50. Several different treatments of shrimp: garlic, pepper, ginger, sweet-and-sour. Siam duck in a heavy, fragrant plum sauce. Pork or beef satay (skewered, with peanut sauce). Everything in the $6.95–$7.45 range.

Teacher's

2249 Broadway
787–3500

An American saloon, simple and unpretentious: a lively place for a drink, and a quiet place for lunch.

Yellow Rose Cafe

450 Amsterdam Avenue
595–8760

Texas chilli, barbecued ribs, fried chicken, lumpy mashed potatoes
and cream gravy. A narrow room, faintly chic, friendly, easy-going
service, and in the evenings mostly packed. Your best bet is to leave
your name and step three doors down to the nearest bar for a beer
while you wait. Lunchtime is more peaceful. Open for brunch on
Sundays.

The Village
Caffe Dante

79 MacDougal (just south of Bleecker Street)

Espresso and pastry, and good eavesdropping if you speak Italian.

Casa di Pre

89 Greenwich Avenue (off 12th Street)
242–9255

A pleasant variety of pastas and seafood in the $5.00 to $7.00 range.
The shops on either side have recently fallen to property developers,
a sign of impending doom for this friendly little place – but worth
dropping in if it survives. Open Monday-Saturday, 12.00–2.30 and
5.00 to 10.00. No credit cards.

Chez Brigitte

77 Greenwich Avenue (between Bank Street and Seventh Avenue)
929–6736

Probably the least pretentious French restaurant in the city: nothing
more than a couple of narrow counters. The sign in the window
says 'Chez Brigitte will seat 250 persons, 11 at one time.' Omelettes
and salads run about $3.00; ragoûts and boeuf bourguignon, about
$7.00. High quality, low elbow-room.

Cornelia Street Cafe

29 Cornelia Street
929–9869

A simple, friendly cafe, good for a light meal or an afternoon snack: boudin blanc (a light veal-and-chicken sausage) with lentils vinaigrette and boiled potatoes . . . tortellini salad with green beans and pignolis (pine nuts). Both $5.50. Readings by local poets and fiction writers on occasional Sunday nights.

Cottonwood Cafe

415 Bleecker Street (at Bank Street)
924–6271

A cheerful open place with a Tex-Mex accent. Entrées about $7.00: barbequed chicken, okra, enchiladas, jalapenos . . . and deep-dish apple pie or pecan pie for dessert. From 10.30 to midnight there's live music.

El Faro

823 Greenwich Street (at Horatio Street)
929–-8210

Till recently, cheap and unassuming; now coming up in the world. Their seafood has always been wonderful: Mariscada al ajillo (mixed seafood in a hot garlic sauce) is $8.25; shrimp with saffron rice is $7.50; paella a la Valenciana is $8.25. The bad news is that these are *lunch* prices: dinner entrées will set you back $13.00 to $16.00.

Elephant & Castle

68 Greenwich Avenue (just south of 11th Street)
243–1400

Hundreds of omelettes from $3.00 to $8.00; salads, sandwiches, crepes, burgers: with mozzarella, guacamole, gruyere . . . $5.00 to $7.00. Fancy desserts, exotic sodas. Tin ceiling, panelled walls, warm light, and charming service. A friendly, unpressured place, but not exactly haute cuisine. Branch at 183 Prince Street in SoHo.

Garvin's

19 Waverley Place (east of Washington Square)
473–5261

This room looks like a remnant of the Raj: high ceilings, revolving fans, a pink-and-gold motif. Very relaxing but not cheap. Lunch à la carte – cold tortellini salad, e.g. – is $6.00 to $13.00; dinner – slightly exotic grilled entrées – $11.00–$20.00. I had an utterly delicious and vastly overpriced sandwich of curried chicken breast and avocado on thin slices of rye – but worth it just for basking privileges.

Grand Ticino

228 Thompson Street
777–5922

One of the great surviving Italian restaurants of the Village. A large, slightly subterranean room, dark green walls, subdued light, and a collection of courtly, veteran waiters who know their business and enjoy it. An immense antipasto is $6.50. Linguine with white clam sauce, $7.50; exquisite scallopine with Marsala, $8.50. The zabaglione – hot liquid custard made with egg and marsala – is out of this world. They don't take reservations (and they'll inform you that reservations aren't necessary) but it can be crowded, so go early in the evening. AE only.

Graziella

2 Bank Street (at Greenwich Avenue)

Antipasti from $4.00 to $6.00, and pastas (including tortellini and canneloni) are about $8.00: they do a very charming Spaghetti alla Puttanesca: tomatoes, garlic, olives, capers. Scallopine Vincenzo – with mushrooms and cream – is $12.75.

Greenwich Time

108 Greenwich Avenue
807–8329

Greenwich Avenue seems to hold the New York monopoly for tiny restaurants. This one is minute, but it does have tables. Eclectic

French/Italian cuisine: fusili Bolognese ($7.95) juxtaposed with chicken dijonais ($8.95); crab remoulade ($4.95) and penne foreste pasta (with wild mushrooms and cream sauce – $7.95). Plus a startling variety of veal and fish dishes: where do they keep it all? Open for dinner only, seven days.

John's Pizzeria

278 Bleecker Street
243–1680

Pizza (the best). Aficionados of John's, and those of Ray's (see below) are the Montagues and Capulets of New York. You'll have to decide for yourself. Thin crust, perfect accoutrements, dismal surroundings, a line in front, and incredible pizza.

Paris Commune

411 Bleecker Street (between West 11th Street and Bank Street)
929–0509

I had a fine mustard-glazed breast of chicken here, served with a salad, for $9.75: that night's special. The menu is otherwise undistinguished – fettucine and such in the $7.00 range, and the P.C. reverts to burgers for lunch, about $6.00. A cosy, subdued interior, and friendly treatment.

Pink Teacup

42 Grove Street (just west of Seventh Avenue)

A Harlem emigrant to the Village. The name is to be taken literally – the place is rosy inside and about as big as a teacup. The Teacup serves soulfood staples: Virginia ham, pigs' feet, pork chops and fried chitterlings, with prices ranging from $6.00 to $11.00. Vegetables follow suit: lima beans, black-eyed peas, rice, greens, yellow turnips, okra, corn and tomatoes. Homesick southerners can breakfast here on chops and fritters for $7.50, or have sausages and eggs with hominy grits for $6.50. The food is abundant – one order is enough for two normal humans; and the service is friendly, chatty and easy-going. They like their customers 'quick and sassy'.

Ray's Pizza

11th Street & Sixth Avenue
243–2253

See John's above. Terrific pizza for aficionados of the thick-crusted south-of-Rome variety. You can feed four people for about $12.

Rocco

181 Thompson Street
677–0590

A Neapolitan holdout in the Village, with a standard but wide-ranging menu: manicotti (pronounced *manigót* in these parts), ravioli, lasagne, canneloni all at $7.50 (and the canelloni are superb); various scallopine (pizzaiola, marsala, al limone) at $9.95; occasional exotica: chicken scarpariello? Tortellini al Gorgonzola? I was afraid to ask.

Sazerac House

533 Hudson Street (at Charles Street)
989–0313

Further adventures in fancy Creole cooking: Chicken étouffé, jambalaya, shrimp-crab-and-okra gumbo, from $7.95 to $10.95; and for casual chow, barbequed po-boys. Open from 4.00 p.m. to 1.00 a.m.

Trattoria da Alfredo

90 Bank Street (at West 11th Street)
243–9260

A bright, airy room but not big enough to contain the local pasta-lovers. Superb fettucine and spaghettine: $9.00–$9.75. Closed Tuesdays.

Yorkville
Mocca

1588 Second Avenue (between 82nd and 83rd Streets)
734–6470

'Basic' Hungarian food served in a large, nondescript room with mirrored walls: goulash, chicken or veal paprikasch, home-made noodles ('neckerl'). Plain, pleasant food, incredibly cheap. At lunch, a knot of Hungarian-speakers clustered near the kitchen. Of the same ilk, but slightly more elegant (and expensive), are:
Budapest Cafe
1373 First Avenue (at 74th Street)
772–8508
and
Csardas
1477 Second Avenue (between 77th and 78th Streets)
472–3892

Wall Street
Chrisa's Cafe

78 Pearl Street
344–6900

People don't eat in Wall Street – they grab a bite. Chrisa's is the exception: a bright, cheerful place to have lunch. The food is undistinguished Greek – but cheap, and a much better bet than scavenging for lunch in the South Street Seaport, up the street. Appetizers – spanikopita (spinach and feta in filo pastry), taramasalata (a sort of roe dip), hommos (addictive chick pea concoction) from $2.85 to $3.25. Main courses – kefte kebab or pastitsio (baked lamb and pasta), for example – are under $6.00; souvlaki is $3.25.

Festivals – ethnic food – hand-held – food 'to go'

New Yorkers probably are no more food-obsessed than anyone else – they only seem so because they're such public eaters. If they're not actually in a restaurant, they're motivating down Broadway with the dog's leash in one hand and a giant pretzel in the other. One theory is that Manhattan apartments are so small that the citizens are driven to dine out, preferably *al fresco*; my guess is they just love an audience. Here is what you'll see on city streets:

Street food

Bagels
The old-fashioned kind are 'water bagels' – boiled after they're shaped, then baked and stored for several hours after they come out of the oven. They provide employment for the jaws. The modern variety are lighter and spongier. From street vendors. For 24-hour bagels:

H&H Bagels
2239 Broadway (at 80th Street)
Baked on the premises and 40 cents apiece, with lowering of the fee structure after the eleventh one. I'm partial to the poppy-seed variety; you can also get plain, pumpernickel, various other incarnations. Open 24 hours.

Hot roasted chestnuts
You'll find these, beginning with the first snap of winter, on Fifth Avenue from about St Patrick's (50th Street) to the lower reaches of Central Park, and on the steps of the Library and the Metropolitan. On a bitter day, they'll warm your pockets as well as your spirits.

Frankfurters
Sabrett and Hebrew National are the best known and most reliable mainstays of the *déjeuner sur l'herbe* crowd. Look for the big yellow umbrellas on pushcarts at the more populous edges of Central Park and in office-building plazas.

Orange juice
Fresh squeezed. New Yorkers drink lakes of it, as well as grapefruit juice, pineapple juice, papaya juice . . . For some reason you'll find most of the vendors in subway and railroad stations, as well as a few on upper Broadway.

Pizza
By the slice, from hole-in-the-wall vendors, or in the bigger subway stations: Times Square, Grand Central. Far from gourmet but, pizza standards being what they are in New York, better than what you'll find out of town. For *inspired* pizza, go to John's or Ray's in the Village (pp.98–99).

Pistachios
The salty little red-shelled ones which stain your fingers. One or two vendors on Fifth Avenue in the 50s.

Pretzels
The 'street' variety of pretzels is big, salty and spongy on the inside. Preferably eaten hot, and excellent refurbishment on cold days, when you're burning galaxies of carbohydrates.

Plus: Argentinian empanadas, Mexican tacos and tostadas, Syrian falafel-stuffed pita, West Indian roti, Greek souvlaki, scattered in storefronts, subway stalls and stands all over town.

Food 'to go'

Baskin Robbins, Haagen-Dazs, Frusen Glädjé
Numerous store-front outlets for ice cream exotica. Choice of cone: 'sugar' (pointed end, dark brown, crisp) or 'plain' (*also* known as 'cake', 'flat', 'wafer', 'cup' or 'regular' – sawdust). There's also a little gourmet number called a Dove Bar which you can buy from street vendors in midtown, for a small fortune.

Buttercake Squares Inc.
Madison Avenue between 82nd and 83rd Streets
Wonderful jam-filled pastries – perfect for a post-Museum pick-me-up – baked and sold in a little tiled (scarcely visible) alcove on the west side of the block.

Habey's Cookies
73 West 83rd Street (just east of Columbus)
Alluring Southern cookies. Try 'Habey's Babies'.

In a Basket
226 East 83rd Street (between 2nd and 3rd Avenues)
472–9787
Included here solely on the basis of aroma, charm and friendliness
– I haven't actually laid hands on their herbed chicken. They cater
for picnics, down to the hamper.

Mrs Field's Cookies
2086 Broadway (at 72nd Street)
Mind-expanding. Especially the Macadamia Nut-Chocolate Chips.
If you don't find yourself in Mrs Field's neighbourhood at the exact
moment of weakness, try one of the ubiquitous branches of David's
Cookies.

Paradise Market
1100 Madison Avenue (at 83rd Street)
Exotic fruits and vegetables, enticingly displayed, and appropriately
located in this boulevard of high-ticket art.

Zabar's
2245 Broadway (at 80th Street)
11 a.m. on a weekday is the ideal time to hit Zabar's, the ultimate
Upper West Side deli cornucopia. On weekends, the staff are in a
state of maximum harassment, and it's fun only if you like being
chivvied through queues by the upwardly mobile.

Pastry
The genres of pastry tend to obey neighbourhood demarcations:
strudel at the Rigo Bakery, in Hungarian Yorkville; cannoli and
panettone at Rocco's on Bleecker Street, in Little Italy; croissants
and brioches at Dumas or Bonté, on the Upper East Side; mandel-
brot and kichels at Moishe's, in the Lower East Side. Stop wherever
the craving takes you.

Dim sum
Little pillows of steamed dough, filled with minced pork and
vegetables – or minced spare ribs, shrimp or duck's feet, crab claws,
roast pork, etc., ad infinitum. Getting fed is fairly haphazard: in
the more chaotic dim sum emporia, you beat the crowds to a table,
then wait till a waiter passes by with a cart. Point to whatever looks
interesting and, with luck, by the time you've finished that round,
someone will come by with another cart. When you're about ready
to die of dim sum, the waiter tallies the plates and calculates. By
nosing around the Mott Street neighbourhood, you'll find any
number of dim sum palaces. Here are a few:

Golden Gate Coffee Shop, 57 Bayard Street
HSF, 46 Bowery
Mee Sum Coffee Shop, 26 Pell Street
Mee Sum Mee Tea House and Pastry, 48 Mott Street
Nom Wah, 13 Doyers Street
Wah Loon Coffee Shop, 13 Chatham Square (at Doyers Street)

Lower East Side Specialities:

Yonah Schimmel's Knishes
137 East Houston Street

A knish is a thin pastry crust wrapped, usually, around potatoes but sometimes kasha, or a meat filling, or what-have-you. Baked, not fried. Absolutely basic and loaded with nostalgia. Yonah Schimmel's has been selling them since 1910.

Russ and Daughters
179 East Houston Street
Lox – especially lox – and smoked whitefish, pickled salmon, pickled herring in sour cream with onion rings, schmaltz herring, home-made gefilte fish. And low prices on caviare.

Moishe's Bakery
181 East Houston Street
Bialys (onion rolls), bagels, challah (braided egg bread) and Jewish rye.

Ben's Cheese Shop
181 East Houston Street
Kosher farmer's cheese in all flavours: even fruit-flavoured cheeses.

Economy Candy
131 Essex Street
The place to buy candy by the bushel. If you're up to nothing more than a quick bite, try the halvah: plain or marbled with chocolate.

Guss & Hollander's Pickles
35 Essex Street
Sours (briny) and half-sours (new pickles). Plus pickled tomatoes, sauerkraut and fresh horseradish just before Passover.

Festival food
Ninth Avenue International Festival

Third weekend in May.

Ninth Avenue – the Clinton neighbourhood – abounds with produce and imported food markets: the greatest among them is Manganaro's (at 37th Street), the nonpareil importer of Italian delicacies . . . but you'll find everything from banana leaves to phyllo dough in the shops along Ninth. The annual International Festival brings the goods, and the multitudes, out into the middle of the avenue for a strolling banquet of hand-held food.

Italian street festivals

Early June: Feast of St Anthony of Padua (Sullivan and West Houston Street, and on Thompson Street between Grand and Canal Streets)

Mid-July: Feast of Our Lady of Mt Carmel (114th–116th Streets, east of First Avenue)

Late July: Feast of Our Lady of Pompeii (Carmine Street)

Mid-September: Feast of San Gennaro (Mulberry Street between Spring and Canal Streets)

San Gennaro (the patron saint of Naples) has the biggest and best-attended of the *feste*. At dusk, the street becomes an arcade of coloured lights and the incense of hot oil and garlic rises from the sidewalk stands. There's plenty of entertainment (the crowds not least) but the main event here is food: cold clams on the half shell with hot pepper sauce; skewered sausages and peppers, charcoal grilled; crude Calabrian pizza with tomato paste and basil; calzone ('big socks') filled with ricotta, mozzarella, salami, prosciutto, deep-fried; zeppole, showered in sugar and lemon, blisteringly hot; citron and ricotta-filled cannoli; multi-layered sfogliatelle stuffed with custard and bitter cherries.

Saloon society

New York has singles bars, gay bars, Madison Avenue agency bars, literary bars, ethnic bars, piano bars, stockbrokers' bars, any number of 'legendary' bars: bars for just about everyone but unaccompanied minors. There are even a couple of pubs – or bars that call themselves pubs. But New Yorkers aren't particularly social drinkers – they tend to congregate in twos, or carry on heart-to-hearts with the bartender, or keep an eye on the Mets between belts. There's a solemnity – a seriousness of purpose – in all but the most frivolous of the city's bars.

If you patronize the saloons, you'd best stick to wine and spirits: you'll find most American beer unspeakable. Most of it seems to have originated in the Germanic midwest (Wisconsin is the culprit), and all brands taste about the same to British palates: thin, bland, hypercarbonated and all but frozen. 'Lite' (low-calorie) and 'L.A.' (low-alcohol) beer are recent inventions, and people actually drink them. Import lagers, such as Heineken and Becks, are universally sold – even exclusively sold in certain ritzy bars – and it's occasionally possible to get hold of a bottle of Watney's or Bass, at the correct temperature if you're lucky.

American domestic wines have come up in the world in the last few years, and some are excellent. The prices have risen with the quality, and a French import is quite often a better buy than a California or New York State wine. If you enjoy window-shopping for wine, try:

Acker, Merrall & Condit

2373 Broadway (between 86th and 87th Streets)

Astor Wine & Spirits

12 Astor Place (at Lafayette and 8th Streets)

A wine supermarket, complete with carts.

Sherry-Lehmann Wine & Spirits

679 Madison Avenue (between 61st and 62nd Streets)

The grand seigneur of New York wine merchants.

Americans are very fanciful when it comes to ordering spirits. Mixed drinks run to the bizarre, even the murderous: zombies, B-52s, kamikazes. Some technical terms:

Neat = in a shot glass, unadulterated
Straight up = no ice
On the rocks = on ice
Back = on the side
With a twist = with a twist of lemon or lime
A double = large

New York's professional drinkers refer to New Year's Eve as Amateur Night. The one other occasion when it's difficult not to be swept into a saloon is Saint Patrick's Day. If you're English, this is a good day to stay *out* of Irish bars: no one is more nationalistic than New York's third-generation Irish.

A few saloon possibilities:

McSorley's Old Ale House

15 East 7th Street (between Second and Third Avenues)
473–8800

A bar of the sawdust-floor variety, now a watering-place for the young. Until 1971, women were not admitted, and the liberation of McSorley's – achieved simultaneously with the opening of the Oak Room at the Plaza to women – was a famous victory for feminists in New York.

Great Jones Street Cafe

54 Great Jones Street (1 block south of East 4th Street)
674–9304

A revisionist Bowery saloon: very small, and always hopping. Simple southern food: burgers and barbecue, blackened redfish. Great Jones Street, just off the Bowery, is one of the city's former showcases, badly battered over the years, but with hopes of revitalization. The Jones is identifiable by its bright orange front and the word 'Jones' above the door. Open from 5:00 p.m. on, and packed.

The Odeon

145 West Broadway
233–0507

A perfectly good saloon, formerly a TriBeCa cafeteria, now full of the well-dressed and well-off, but by all accounts a dismal place to have dinner. Bianca Jagger is said to have stormed out in pique over the food.

Corner Bistro

331 West 4th Street (at Jane Street)
242–9502

A *basic* bar with a great jazz and rock juke box, booths in the back (for cheap *basic* burgers), and a friendly, slightly sodden crowd up front: no frills. Noisy and happy. The kitchen stays open till 4.00 a.m.

Lion's Head

59 Christopher Street (at Seventh Avenue)
929–0670

An old hangout for *Village Voice* reporters.

White Horse Tavern

567 Hudson Street (at West 11th Street)
243–9260

The White Horse's claim to fame is that Dylan Thomas drank himself to death here. Despite that, it's not a bad bar.

Cedar Tavern

82 University Place (between 11th and 12th Streets)
929–9089

An artists' saloon of yesteryear, with an elaborate bar that could have been transported piece by piece from St Patrick's Cathedral, and two-fisted drinks. There's reputed to be a glassed-in restaurant on the roof, and there are plenty of tables in the back – I had a delicious salade niçoise for lunch here one day – but the Cedar's true vocation is to serve humanity as a saloon.

Chumley's

86 Bedford Street
675–4449

New York's only surviving speakeasy, as well hidden now as it was during Prohibition. This used to be a writers' hangout, and the walls are still covered with their book jackets. Free juke box and lively crowd.

City lights:
Exhibits and performances

Art

Sometime in the 1950s – arguably even before that – the art capital of the world shifted to New York, and it has remained there obstinately ever since. New York sets the standards by which contemporary art is judged; it seems to be impelled to prove itself in the vanguard by testing new ground at all times: consequently, the public is under a constant barrage of the extreme, the incongruous, the outrageous, the untried. It's an arena of overnight traditions: schools of art which spring up overnight and evaporate by late afternoon. A stroll through some of the more strategic clusters of galleries will give you an instant insight into what will be going on in art for the next 24 hours.

The museums, by and large, are stately, serene, relatively changeless – and anything but dusty repositories of dead art. New Yorkers flock to see their treasures. The Metropolitan Museum on a Sunday is like Grand Central Station at rush hour. The Modern Museum is like a giant cocktail party without the canapés. If you're there to look at art rather than people, the off-hours – early weekday mornings, except Monday – will give you the clearest view.

Most museums have a 'suggested' admission charge, on the principle that the really down-and-out should not be denied access to art. As long as the cost of admission doesn't actually take bread out of your mouth, you should pay the full fare.

Museums (and everything else) close for major holidays: Independence Day (4 July), Thanksgiving Day (fourth Thursday in November), Christmas Day and New Year's Day. Most museums stay open late, with free admission, on Tuesday evenings; and most are closed Mondays. If in doubt a phone call will save you a wasted trip.

Museums and Collections
American Craft Museum

77 West 45th Street (International Paper Plaza)
371–8770

Hours: Monday–Saturday, 10.00 a.m.–5.00 p.m.
Admission: General, $1.50; Children/Senior Citizens, $.75
Glass, wood, textiles, basketry, paper, pottery.

Asia Society

725 Park Avenue (at 70th Street)
288–6400

Hours: Tuesday–Saturday, 11.00 a.m.–6.00 p.m. Sunday,
noon–5.00 p.m. Closed Mondays
Admission: General, $2; Students, $1

Houses the Rockefeller collection of Asian art – small and select,
mostly sculpture and pottery. Two Japanese prints are on display,
out of a collection of four, and pieces of Korean and Chinese
celadon: the Korean a darker, bluer shade. The Society offers inten-
sive (and expensive) courses on a wide range of topics; an array of
Asian music, dance, theatre and puppetry performances; regular
film showings, special art exhibitions and lectures on innumerable
aspects of Asia.

Brooklyn Museum

188 Eastern Parkway
Prospect Park, Brooklyn
718–638–5000

Hours: Monday, Wednesday, Thursday, Friday:
10.00 a.m.–5.00 p.m. Saturday: 11.00 a.m.–6.00 p.m. Sunday:
1.00–6.00 p.m. Closed Tuesdays.
Admission: General, $2; Students, $1; Senior Citizens and
accompanied children under 12, free
Subway: Broadway – 7th Avenue IRT express to Eastern
Parkway/Brooklyn Museum stop

Period rooms from the 18th and 19th centuries; an excellent decorative arts collection; permanent and special collections.

The Cloisters

Fort Tryon Park
923–3700

Transport: Madison Avenue bus no. 4 ('The Cloisters–Fort Tryon Park') or Eighth Avenue subway to 190th Street – Overlook Terrace and walk through the park.
Hours: Tuesday–Sunday 9.30 a.m.–5.15 p.m. (March–October); 9.30 a.m.–4.45 p.m. (November–February); Closed Mondays
Admission: $4 (includes admission to the Metropolitan Museum)

The Metropolitan Museum's branch for medieval art, at the northern tip of Manhattan. Built in the 1930s, and incorporates sections of a 12th-century chapter house, parts of cloisters from five medieval monasteries, a Romanesque chapel, and a 12th-century Spanish apse. The stonework, the architectural details, the stained glass, the wood- and stone-carved sculpture, and especially the tapestries, are stunning. The showpieces are three arcaded French cloister gardens, each of a different period and region, and each with its special plantings.

One of the delights of the Cloisters is its concert scries, which runs between October and April, and emphasizes medieval and Renaissance music. Tickets are available by mail only. You can pick up an order form at the Cloisters, or write to Concerts/The Cloisters, Fort Tryon Park, New York, NY 10040.

Cooper-Hewitt Museum

2 East 91st Street (at Fifth Avenue)
860–6898

Hours: Tuesday, 10.00 a.m.–9.00 p.m. Wednesday–Saturday, 10.00 a.m.–5.00 p.m. Sunday, 12.00 p.m.–5.00 p.m.
Admission: Adults, $2 (free on Tuesday evenings)

The Smithsonian Institution's National Museum of Design, housed in the Andrew Carnegie manse. An immense collection of drawings and myriad objets d'art; excellent special exhibitions.

Frick Collection

1 East 70th Street (at Fifth Avenue)
288–0700

Hours: Tuesday–Saturday, 10.00 a.m.–6.00 p.m. Sunday:
1.00 p.m.–6.00 p.m. Closed Mondays, Independence Day,
Thanksgiving, Christmas Eve and Christmas Day, and New Year's
Day.
Admission: General, $1 Tuesday–Saturday; $2 on Sundays;
Students/Senior Citizens, 50¢
Children under 10 are not admitted to the Collection; those under
16 must be accompanied by an adult.

A private house in 18th-century period style, built around the turn
of the century by a Pittsburgh industrialist. Inside are treasures
that will leave you stunned: Rembrandt, Vermeer, Chardin,
Gainsborough, Titian, Goya, Velázquez, Ingres, Turner, Boucher;
Holbein's portraits of More and Cromwell; a room full of Fragon-
ards; and much more, packed into a jewel-like house with a garden
court and ornamental pool at its heart. If your time in New York
is limited to one event, this should be the one.

Guggenheim Museum

Fifth Avenue at 89th Street
360–3500

Hours: Tuesday, 11.00 a.m.–8.00 p.m. Wednesday–Sunday,
11.00 a.m.–5.00 p.m. Closed Mondays
Admission: General, $2.50; Students, $1.50. Free on Tuesday
evenings

Frank Lloyd Wright's spiral ramp, windowless outside but full of
light from its central dome. Worth visiting even if there's nothing
you're desperate to see at the museum. You take the elevator to the
top and follow the exhibition downhill. Temporary exhibitions line
the inner surface of the spiral, and you're forced to look at the show
from top to bottom – very much Wright's autocratic style. The
Thannhauser collection, in a side gallery about three turns down
from the top, is small but priceless: Lautrec's *Au Salon*, a Modigliani
nude, Cézannes, and works by Degas, Vuillard, Gauguin . . . and
plenty of Picassos.

International Center of Photography

1130 Fifth Avenue (at 94th Street)
860–1777

Hours: Tuesday, noon–8.00 p.m. Wednesday–Friday,
noon–5.00 p.m. Saturday–Sunday, 11.00 a.m.–6.00 p.m.
Admission: General, $2; Students/Senior Citizens, $1; Free on
Tuesday evenings

An elegant townhouse, vintage 1914, beautifully remodelled into
exhibition space: and the exhibitions, contemporary and historical,
are excellent.

Isamu Noguchi Garden Museum

32–37 Vernon Blvd., Long Island City
718–204–7088

Hours: By appointment, Wednesday–Saturday, noon–5.00 p.m.
Transport: Take the RR subway from 59th Street to Broadway
(Astoria). Head west (toward the Manhattan skyline) to Vernon
Boulevard. The museum is two blocks to your left.

Newly opened indoor and outdoor gardens housing the works of
the great sculptor and designer: calm and refreshing.

Jewish Museum

Fifth Avenue at 92nd Street
860–1888

Admission: General, $2.50; Students/Children/Senior Citizens,
$1.50
Hours: Monday–Thursday, noon–5.00 p.m. Tuesday,
noon–8.00 p.m. Friday, 11.00 a.m.–3.00 p.m. Sunday,
11.00 a.m.–6.00 p.m. Closed Saturdays

Collection and exhibitions of work by and about New York's largest
'minority'. Everything from contemporary painting to a theme-show
on the great Jewish art patrons of Venice.

The Metropolitan Museum of Art

Fifth Avenue at 82nd Street

Hours: Wednesday-Sunday, 9.30 a.m.–5.15 p.m. Tuesday,
9.30 a.m.–8.45 p.m. Closed Mondays
Admission: General, $4; Students/Senior Citizens, $2; Children
under 12, accompanied by an adult, free
Information: Concerts and lectures: 570–3949 for tickets;
744–9120 for recorded information
Other information: 535–7710

Mammoth and comprehensive: everything from King Tut's tomb
to the 20th century. Notable departments: the Costume Institute
(plaything of Diana Vreeland, who used to run Vogue); the Egyp-
tian Wing is the latest in museum design. Our current favourite is
the American Wing, with its Sargents, Cassatts and Eakins – but
we could just as easily get involved in the Cézannes in the Post-
Impressionist gallery. The Michelin 'green guide' to New York
and the *Blue Guide* have concise but comprehensive notes to the
collections, and might be useful if you were in a rush to see certain
things – but ultimately it doesn't pay to rush through the Met.

The Museum Cafeteria is open from 9.30 to 10.30 a.m. (for continental breakfast) and from 11.00 a.m. to 4.30 p.m. Tuesday–Sunday
(and 5.00–8.00 p.m. Tuesday). At some point you'll need a
breather, and if the weather won't let you sit on the front steps, the
cafeteria is your best bet.

Museum of American Folk Art

125 West 55th Street
581–2474

Hours: Tuesday, 10.30 a.m.–8.00 p.m. Wednesday–Sunday,
10.30 a.m.–5.30 p.m. Closed Monday
Admission: General, $2; Students/Senior Citizens, $1; Free on
Tuesday evenings

American primitives on the order of Grandma Moses.

Museum of American Illustration

128 East 63rd Street (between Park and Lexington Avenues)
838–2560

Hours: Monday–Friday, 10.00 a.m.–5.00 p.m. Tuesday,
10.00 a.m.–8.00 p.m.
Admission: Free

Display space for members and mentors of the American Society of
Illustrators: in the downstairs gallery a variety of magazine and
advertising art from the Society's collection; on the ground floor a
major show: a mammoth collection of Paul Davis paintings and
cover art when last visited.

Museum of Modern Art

11 West 53rd Street (between Fifth and Sixth Avenues)

Hours: Daily, 11.00 a.m.–6.00 p.m. Thursday,
11.00 a.m.–9.00 p.m. Closed Wednesdays and Christmas Day
Admission: General, $4.50; Students, $3; Senior Citizens, $2.
Children under 16, accompanied by an adult, free.
Information: Current exhibitions: 708–9480
Film showings: 708–9490
Other information: 708–9400

MOMA, as it's affectionately known, has the most comprehensive
collection of 20th-century painting and sculpture in the world: all
the major schools, from post-Impressionism to the present day. Plus
incredible collections of 20th-century photography, prints, drawings, and an Architecture and Design collection with more than
5000 examples of furniture, household items, tools, posters and

what-have-you. It's also one of the very best places in the city to watch people. New Yorkers regularly use the Modern as a refuge from the hassles of midtown: the sculpture garden is an oasis of peace, and it's possible to lose yourself for half an hour in a room full of Monet waterlilies. Weekdays, before or after lunch, are the best time to avoid the crowds.

MOMA also has a fabulous film collection, and screens up to thirty movies a week, free with admission (the theatre fills up fast, so get there early). The Garden Café, for light meals and self-service snacks, is open from 11.00 a.m.–4.30 p.m. (8.00 p.m. on Thursday). It's not super-cheap, but you can spot local celebs there (the Mayor, for example) on occasion, and it can be a lifesaver after a hard morning amid all that art.

National Academy of Design

1083 Fifth Avenue (at 89th Street)
369–4880

Hours: Tuesday, noon–8.00 p.m. Wednesday–Sunday,
noon–5.00 p.m. Closed Mondays;
Admission: General, $2, Children/Senior Citizens, $1.50; Free on
Tuesday evenings

A Beaux-Arts mansion full of fairly staid examples of American art, but with occasional surprises: a collection of Sargent drawings in June 1985, and an Edward Lear exhibit in October.

New Museum of Contemporary Art

583 Broadway (between Houston and Prince Streets)
219–1222

Hours: Wednesday, noon–8.00 p.m. Thursday–Sunday,
noon–6.00 p.m. Closed Mondays and Tuesdays
Admission: General, $2.50; Artists, Students and Senior Citizens,
$1.50; Children under 12, free

Three floors of ex-industrial space in SoHo devoted to the new, the startling, and the evanescent. A lively place to visit. Solo shows, and three subsidiary installations: the New Work Gallery features works by artists who 'have not received significant exposure' in New York City; Workspace, on the second floor, used for 'site-specific installations' and small exhibitions; and the Window, 'an installation space that wilfully engages the general public'. In autumn 1985 it was an ant farm, eye level, on Broadway.

Pierpont Morgan Library

29 East 36th Street
685–0008

Hours:Tuesday–Saturday, 10.30 a.m.–5.00 p.m. Sunday,
1.00–5.00 p.m. Closed Mondays, Sundays in July, and the month of August.
Admission: $3

J. P. Morgan's sumptuous marble library, full of artistic, historical and literary collections. Bits and pieces are always on view: medieval and Renaissance manuscripts, drawings, autograph manuscripts, letters, musical scores. There are several major exhibitions per year: the star of 1985 was a stupendous collection of prints from the Albertina Palace in Vienna. The Morgan is low on mass-appeal – it attracts an elegant, scholarly clientele, and has a special appeal to connoisseurs of the endless variety of New York crowds.

The Studio Museum in Harlem

144 West 125th Street
864–4500

Hours: Wednesday–Friday, 10.00 a.m.–5.00 p.m.
Saturday–Sunday, 1.00 p.m.–6.00 p.m. Closed Mondays and Tuesdays
Admission: General, $1.50; Children, 50¢

Harlem's museum, with works primarily by black artists, primarily on black themes and issues.

Whitney Museum of American Art

945 Madison Avenue (at 75th Street)
570–3600

Hours: Wednesday–Saturday, 11.00 a.m.–5.00 p.m. Tuesday,
1.00 p.m.–8.00 p.m. Sundays and holidays, noon–6.00 p.m.
Admission: General, $3; Senior Citizens, $1.50; Free on Tuesdays from 6.00 to 8.00 p.m.

Some delights of the permanent collection: a Lachaise *Standing Woman*; paintings by O'Keeffe, Hopper, Demuth; George Bellows's eyewitness painting of the 1923 Dempsey-Firpo fight. Works by de Kooning, Lichtenstein, Jasper Johns, and their contemporaries. And major exhibitions of current American art. The building is by Marcel Breuer: heavily cantilevered, with asymmetrical windows – its pleasures include a sunken garden and immense carpeted freight elevators for the public. A new addition by the 'neo-classical' architect, Michael Graves, is in the works.

Galleries

Galleries are essentially art shops: they don't charge admission, and they do want you to buy things. But even if you never spend a cent on art, by merely walking in and glancing around you have the potential to help establish the reputation of each gallery's 'stable' of artists. Hence, a rule-of-thumb: no matter how formidable the exterior of a gallery, or how stuck-up the hired help, there's no reason why you shouldn't spend half an hour perusing whatever covers the walls.

There are almost as many galleries in New York as there are restaurants, and no one can begin to list them all. Some (like restaurants) have life-spans numbered in weeks, and I haven't tried to scout these out: you'll stumble across them on your own if you're interested. The following include samplings of the city's 'establishment' galleries as well as those on the leading edge. Most are open Tuesday–Saturday, from about 10.00 a.m. to 6.00 p.m., and many close for a month or two in summer.

If you're not in search of a specific gallery or artist, it's generally simpler to pick one of the three areas of town most densely packed with art: Madison Avenue, 57th Street and SoHo.

Upper Madison Avenue, 57th to 81st Streets

A good place to buy a Matisse drawing or a Vlaminck still life. Some galleries are inclined to stuffiness, but if you can get past that, there are great surprises. There is also a lot of expensive schlock, but a glance in the window will keep keep you from wasting your time.

ACA

21 East 67th Street

Specializes in 20th-century American art: O'Keeffe, Benton, Marsh, Social Realism, the Ashcan School, the Stieglitz Group.

David Findlay

984 Madison Avenue, at 77th Street

Established 1870. 19th- and 20th-century European and American painting, sculpture, graphics.

Graham

1014 Madison Avenue (at 78th Street, 2nd floor)

Contemporary and late 19th-20th century American painters.

Hoffeld

1020 Madison Avenue (at 79th Street, 5th floor)

Recently: an extraordinary show of women Surrealists, 1930–50.

Isselbacher

41 East 78th Street (off Madison Avenue)

European prints: Matisse lithographs, on our last visit.

M. Knoedler

19 East 70th Street

Mostly American art, Whistler to the present, with emphasis on the Abstract Expressionists.

Perls

1016 Madison Avenue (at 79th Street)

Limited to School of Paris – if that can be considered a limit. Examples: a superb Vlaminck vase with pink buds; a delectable

Pascin; one of Matissé's lightning conté portraits; a pencilled Modigliani nude.

Ronin

605 Madison Avenue (between 57th and 58th Streets, upstairs)

Japanese prints in profusion.

Solomon

959 Madison Avenue (at 75th Street)

Calder, Dubuffet, Frankenthaler, Lindner, Rothko.

Staempfli

47 East 77th Street

Contemporary American, European, Asian painting and sculpture.

Wildenstein

19 East 64th Street

A rather grand gallery. Old masters, Impressionists, contemporary art.

57th Street, Park Avenue to Sixth Avenue

Established galleries with contemporary stables, or the reins on artists' estates. Nothing you see here will be experimental, and everything will be expensive by any standards. Window shopping doesn't work: most of the galleries are in the narrow, older buildings, on the upper floors. The mainstream of American art is concentrated here.

Terry Dintenfass

50 West 57th Street

Contemporary American.

Emmerich

41 East 57th Street

Contemporary American: Morris Louis for example. Also some David Hockncy.

Fishbach

29 West 57th Street

Realist painting.

Sidney Janis

110 West 57th Street

Blockbuster shows of 20th-century and contemporary art: everything from Piet Mondrian to Saul Steinberg.

Marlborough

40 West 57th Street

Modern and contemporary art and photography. Red Grooms's 'comic' installations show up here occasionally. Recently: Schwitters.

Pierre Matisse

41 East 57th Street

Modern and contemporary Europeans, including Balthus and Dubuffet.

Pace

32 East 57th Street

Recently: Calder sculpture and mobiles. For thrills: Lucas Samaras.

Betty Parsons

24 West 57th Street

American Abstract Expressionism came of age here.

Marilyn Pearl

29 West 57th Street

Contemporary abstracts: a series of 'New Talent' shows.

SoHo

All the vitality of the New York art scene is temporarily here (though there are signs that it's rapidly slopping over into the Lower East Side and TriBeCa). The galleries are housed mostly in the ex-warehouses of West Broadway, which becomes a carnival on Saturday afternoons. Greene Street and Mercer Street are quieter and will give you plenty to look at, architecturally as well as artistically.

Castelli

420 West Broadway and 142 Greene Street

Contemporary painting and resurrected pop artists: new work by Lichtenstein last Spring, for example.

The Drawing Center

137 Greene Street

Works on paper – which can mean *anything* – with one 'theme' show per year. Open Wednesday till 8.00 p.m.

O. K. Harris

383 West Broadway

Mammoth exhibition space and a multitude of solo and group shows.

Phyllis Kind

139 Spring Street

Emphasis on funky American naif art: the Chicago School, if there is such a thing.

Let There Be Neon

451 West Broadway

And there was neon.

Oil & Steel

157 Chambers Street (TriBeCa)

Mark di Suvero, for example: steel sculpture with swinging elements. An extraordinary gallery.

Holly Solomon

392 West Broadway

Performance pieces and installations that stretch the definitions of art. 'Pattern' pieces – from wallpaper to wallpaper-music. Laurie Anderson is a member of the stable.

Sonnabend

420 West Broadway

Demonstrates the ability to be trendy and established simultaneously.

Across the river
P.S. 1

46–01 21st Street, Long Island City

Hours: Thursday–Sunday, noon to 6.00 p.m.

Formerly a public school, currently the leading edge. Transport:

Sixth Avenue IND (F train) to 23rd Street–Ely Avenue in Long Island City (first stop on the other side of the East River).

Street art

Graffiti vs. street art: there is a difference, but it's a fine line. Graffiti are what you see inside the subways – crude signatures defacing every available surface. The slick graphics on the *outside* of subways show a rare flash of brilliance, but by and large they qualify as property damage. It's on the street-level surfaces that something of value sometimes jumps into view:

. . . A cityscape by James Rizzi on outside wall of the Eric Gallery, Second Avenue & 88th Street.

. . . 100 murals by Franco Gaskin (aka the Picasso of Harlem) on the metal riot grates of 125th Street stores. Since these aren't in evidence during business hours, and are scarcely visible at night, you can only see them on Sunday, right?

. . . A hummingbird at 35 Downing Street.

. . . A skyline on the grate of the New York Collision shop, 489 Washington Street.

. . . Mysterious shadow-figures on East 5th Street (and in out-of-the-way places throughout the city) by 'Hugo', last seen somewhere in the Caribbean. These rough splotches of black paint, almost thrown on the city's most derelict walls, are now disappearing under renovations or other people's graffiti. You'll know them when you come across them: powerful, life-size, menacing and anguished.

Music

An abundance of classical music – at a price, as you might expect. For the determined, there are ways to get around this: rehearsals and free concerts abound. Standing-room tickets are sold just before major performances. And half-price tickets for opera, concert and dance performances are available at the Bryant Park Ticket Booth, for same-day seating only, depending on availability. Horowitz's Sunday afternoon performances, for example, are sold out within hours of the first rumour of his appearance.

Bryant Park Ticket Booth
42nd Street east of Sixth Avenue, just inside the park
Hours: Tuesdays–Sunday, noon–7.00 p.m. Wednesdays and
Saturdays, 11.00 a.m.–7.00 p.m.
Tickets for Monday concerts available Sunday prior to performance
date.

The big halls:

Carnegie Hall (and Carnegie Recital Hall)
57th Street and Seventh Avenue
247–7800

The world's best acoustics. Even the cheapest seats are in perfect
earshot of the stage. The range is from about $15 to $35 for big-
time orchestral and solo events, considerably less for Recital Hall
performances.

Grace Rainey Rogers Auditorium
Metropolitan Museum
82nd Street and Fifth Avenue
744–9120

Small (it holds 700) and perfect for chamber music.

Lincoln Center
62nd to 66th Streets (between Amsterdam and Columbus Avenues)
Comprises:

Alice Tully Hall
362–1911
(Recitals and chamber music)

Avery Fisher Hall
874–2424
(New York Philharmonic)

Metropolitan Opera House
362–6000
(The Met and the American Ballet Theater)

New York State Theater
870–5570
(New York City Opera and the New York City Ballet Company)

Tickets at Lincoln Center can be hard to get. Call Center Charge
to put them on plastic: 874–6770.

Merkin Concert Hall
Abraham Goodman House
129 West 67th Street
362–8719

Town Hall
123 West 43rd Street
840–2824

Less grand

Symphony Space
Broadway, at 95th Street
864–5400

92nd Street Y
Lexington Avenue and 92nd Street
427–4410

Deluxe recitals and chamber music: Yo-Yo Ma, the Tokyo and
Guarneri String Quartets, Claudio Arrau, Hermann Prey,
Emmanuel Ax ... Single tickets are in the $12–$20 range, and
advance sell-outs are common, so keep your disappointment within
bounds.

Free or cut-rate

Occasional free concerts:

The Donnell Library Center
20 West 53rd Street

CUNY Graduate Center Auditorium
33 West 42nd Street

Lincoln Center Library
Behind the Metropolitan Opera,
64th Street between Amsterdam and Columbus Ave.

... and others, listed weekly in New York Magazine Music and
Dance Directory.

Rehearsals
NY Philharmonic
Avery Fisher Hall, Lincoln Center
874–2424

Thursdays at 9.45 a.m.

Student and faculty recitals

Juillard School
Lincoln Center Friday-night concerts with the stars of the future. Free.
799–5000

Brooklyn College Conservatory
Gershwin Theater
Flatbush and Nostrand Avenues, Brooklyn
718–434–1900

Third Street Music School Settlement
235 East 11th Street
777–3240

Roosa School of Music
26 Willow Place, Brooklyn
718–875–7371

Concerts in churches

Generally at noon-time on weekdays, and free. An abundance of Sunday-afternoon concerts, and occasional evening performances, usually with a mild admission charge. And a very enjoyable way for the non-devout to spend time in the city's churches with no question of false pretenses. *New York* magazine has excellent weekly listings. A few of the more decorative venues:

Church of the Ascension
Fifth Avenue at 10th Street

Christ and St Stephen's Church
120 West 69th Street

Grace Church
Broadway at 10th Street

Riverside Church
Riverside Drive and 122nd Street

St Ignatius Loyola
84th Street and Park Avenue

St John the Divine
112th Street and Amsterdam Avenue

Temple Emanu-El
65th Street and Fifth Avenue

Trinity Church
Broadway and Wall Street

St Bartholomew's Church
Park Avenue and 50th Street

Trinity Lutheran
67th Street and Central Park West

And . . .

Brooklyn Academy of Music
30 Lafayette Avenue, Brooklyn
718–636–4100

Better known as 'BAM'. A lively mixed-media arena: its annual 'Next Wave' festival, in October, is a performance extravaganza, mixing dance, music, theatre and opera in startling and unpredictable combinations.

Opera in the Park
In the Central Park Bandshell, summer evenings. Listings in the *Times*.

Bargemusic
Fulton Ferry Landing, Brooklyn
718–624–4061

Seasonal waterfront concerts of jazz and chamber music. Admission in the $8 range.

Ethnic and folk music:
Alternative Museum
17 White Street
966–4444

Laotian instrumentals – Balkan folksongs – American Indian vocals, and everything in between. About $8.

Asia Society
725 Park Avenue (at 70th Street)
288–6400

Performance troupes from Japan, Thailand, India and everywhere else on the far side of the Pacific, but pricey: tickets range from $8 to $20.

For some notes on jazz, see City Nights, p.140.

Dance

New York is dance paradise. In residence: Alvin Ailey, Merce Cunningham, Elliot Feld, Martha Graham, Erick Hawkins, Robert Joffrey, José Limon, Murray Louis, Alwin Nikolais, Paul Taylor, Twyla Tharp, many others on the way up. This means thousands of dancers are constantly criss-crossing New York to see each other's work, as well as the companies passing through town. Keep an eye out for studio performances. The most discriminating listings are in *The New Yorker*, the most comprehensive in *New York* Magazine. Some clues:

Ballet Establishment

New York City Ballet Company
New York State Theater, Lincoln Center
870–5570

Tickets from about $5 to $40.

American Ballet Theatre
Metropolitan Opera House
362–6000

Tickets range from about $10 to $50.

Modern and Eclectic Showcases

Brooklyn Academy of Music
30 Lafayette Avenue, Brooklyn
718–636–4100

A mixed bag – from ballet to bizarre.

City Center
131 West 55th Street
246–8989

Ailey and Joffrey are constants; others come and go. The Lar Lubovitch Company is currently in residence.

Joyce Theater
175 Eight Avenue (at 19th Street)
242–0800

A constant parade of great companies.

If you get tired of looking at dancers and want to do some dancing yourself, see City Nights, p.140.

The movies

It's safe to say that, outside of Calcutta, you can see more movies in Manhattan than any place on earth. If mainstream Hollywood releases are your meat, you'll find them in the big multiplex cinemas of Times Square and upper Broadway. The repertory and art houses, reeking of nostalgia, are scattered around town. Admission is generally between $4 and $5. For schedules, see the *Times, New York* Magazine, *The New Yorker*.

For serious buffs

Bleecker Street Cinema and the Agee Room
144 Bleecker Street
674–2560

Cinema 3 at Lincoln Plaza
Broadway at 63rd Street
757–2280

Metro Cinema
2626 Broadway (at 99th Street)
222–1200

A stunning art-deco theatre.

Millenium Film Workshop
66 East 4th Street
673–0090

Museum of Modern Art
11 West 53rd Street
708–9490

Films free with museum admission, but get there early.

For chestnuts, kitsch, and American classics:

Cinema Village
22 East 12th Street
924–3363

Regency
Broadway and 67th Street
724–3700

Thalia
Broadway and 95th Street
222–3370

Theater 80 St Marks
80 St Marks Place
254–7400

Occasional films on diverse subjects:

Asia Society
Park Avenue and 70th Street
288–6400

Admission: $5

Goethe House
1014 Fifth Avenue (at 82nd Street)
744–8310

Free

Japan Society
333 East 47th Street (between First and Second Avenues)
832–155

Admission: $5

New York Public Library
Donnell Branch
20 West 53rd Street
621–0618

Free

Theatre

Peter Sellars, the current wunderkind of the American National Theater, said recently that 'American theater is in smithereens'. Most other countries have a central company to hold things together: the Comédie Francaise, the Noh drama, the Moscow Art Theatre, but there's nothing comparable in the US. What we do have is Broadway, Off-Broadway, Off-off-Broadway, and a miscellany of improv companies, kitchen-sink performance pieces and video malarkey. If these appeal, your best bet is to scrutinize the capsule reviews in *New York* magazine and *The New Yorker* (the more candid of the two), then head for the unlikely rather than the established.

There will be times when you must absolutely disregard this advice: Dustin Hoffman's performance in *Death of a Salesman* was one. And Bill Irwin is a newly-risen Mozart of the pratfall, not to be missed.

Briefly:

The **Broadway** theatres are mostly between Broadway and Eighth Avenue, in the upper 40s and lower 50s. At least 75 per cent of Broadway plays at any given time are musicals, some of them in the depths of long runs.

Off-Broadway occurs primarily in the Village, with a few theatres on the Upper West Side, and a fair number in the lower west 40s. It runs toward works by new American playwrights, established and on-the-way-up. A few slight musicals, some quite good revivals, and a lot of hand-wringing over sexual and other dilemmas.

Off-off-Broadway theatres are sprinkled all over town – from West End Avenue to SoHo. Political satires, Brecht revivals, sagas of multi-ethnic neighbourhood pride.

If you *must* see a Broadway play, get your tickets at a TKTS outlet. Undiscounted Broadway ticket prices are in the $30–$50 range; even off-Broadway plays can run you up to $30. No wonder there are empty seats. TKTS sells the empties at half price, the day of the performance. Call ahead to find out what's available.

TKTS outlets:
Times Square Ticket Center (Broadway, at 47th Street) 354–5800
Hours: Monday–Saturday, 3.00 p.m.–8.00 p.m. Wednesday and
Saturday, noon–2.00 p.m. Sunday, noon–3.00 p.m.
Lower Manhattan Theatre Center
No 2 World Trade Center, Mezzanine
354–5800
Hours: Monday–Saturday, 11.00 a.m.–5.30 p.m.

The city is loaded with repertory and experimental companies. A few of the more interesting ones:

American Jewish Theatre

Plays performed at the 92nd Street Y, 1395 Lexington Avenue
831–8603

American Shakespeare Repertory Company

at Theater 22
54 West 22nd Street
279–9321

If Shakespeare (and maybe Marlowe and Jonson) in fluent Americanese turns you on . . .

Catch a Rising Star

1487 First Avenue (between 77th and 78th Streets)
794–1906

Proving ground for young comics and singers, seven nights a week.

Circle Repertory

99 Seventh Avenue South
924–7100
Last fall, the Talley trilogy by Lanford Wilson: native American theatre.

La Mama E.T.C.

74A East 4th Street (between the Bowery and Second Avenue)
475–7710

Politics, fantasy, avant-gardism in all its manifestations: you're likely to be either delighted or appalled. Meredith Monk is a reigning goddess. Tickets are in the $10 range.

Gramercy Arts Theater

138 East 27th Street (between Park and Lexington Avenues)
889–2850

An amazing little theatre which runs repertory in Spanish. Lorca performances, effective even if your proficiency in Spanish is *nada*. Spanish ballet occasionally. Heavy on the zarzuela, which is slated to replace sushi in the with-it index. Tickets around $15–20.

Equity Library Theater

103rd Street and Riverside Drive
663–2028

Revivals, with tickets on a 'contribution' basis, proceeds going to Actors' Equity, the labour union of the stars.

Public Theater

425 Lafayette Street
598–7150

Joe Papp/New York Shakespeare Festival productions – but not Shakespeare: David Hare, more likely.

Roundabout

100 East 17th Street
420–1883

Ibsen and such. Excellent productions.

Theater for the New City

162 Second Avenue
254–1109

This counts as off-off-Broadway: East Village, low budget ($4 seats), and productions likely to be surreal.

Street Theater

The more established spots: Columbus Circle . . . the steps of the
42nd Street Library and the Metropolitan Museum . . . Father
Demo Square (Bleecker Street and Sixth Avenue). You're likely to
find mimes and comics (and clowns of every other stripe) at these
and other less predictable locations, especially in the high-visibility
time slots. Lunch is prime time. Audience participation is part of
the sport, be advised. Coming out of the Met to find a mime aping
the gait of every passer-by is like eating Sno-Cones after Escoffier,
but it's dessert nonetheless.

Readings: poetry and prose
Cooper Union

Great Hall Programs
41 Cooper Square (7th Street at Third Avenue)
254–6374

125 years of rallies, concerts, lectures, readings and theatrical events
have given Cooper Union a degree of redolence. Around the turn
of the century it was about the only place that New York's teeming
socialists, Trotskyites and anarchists were on speaking terms, and
it was in the Great Hall that they exhorted the masses almost
nightly. Here you can still hang on the words of politicians, poets,
artists, critics, film-makers, journalists and other New York lumi-
naries, and listen to mostly modern music and lots of jazz. Cooper
Union publishes a seasonal schedule of events, and lists its current
doings in the newspapers. Programmes begin at 8.00 p.m.; admission is usually free.

92nd Street 'Y'

Lexington Avenue (at 92nd Street)
427–4410

Constant readings and lectures by artists, journalists, actors, and
politicos of every stripe. The 1985–86 season included Richard
Wilbur, Robert Penn Warren, Peter Shaffer, Gunter Grass, Eugene

Ionesco, Adrienne Rich, Alice Walker, Calvin Trillin, Geraldine Ferraro. And extensive explorations of Jewish religion and culture, with talks by I. B. Singer, Elie Wiesel, Amos Oz. The Y is a treasure.

Symphony Space

2537 Broadway (at 95th Street)
864–5400

Like the 'Y', a mixed-use hall. Occasional big word events in prose and poetry.

Three Lives & Company

154 West 10th Street
741–2069

A distinctly feminist and very calm and beautiful bookstore. Readings, free, 8 p.m., seating as available, by the likes of Alison Lurie and Alice Adams. Drop by the bookstore for a schedule.

Video
Global Village

454 Broome Street
966–7526

Specializes in documentaries. Admission: $3

The Kitchen

59 Wooster Street
925–3615

The Video Viewing Room runs current works – and occasional 'video installations' – by new video artists. Tuesday–Saturday, from 1.00 p.m. to about 6.00 p.m. Free.

Museum of Broadcasting

1 East 53rd Street
752–7684

See listing under Museums, p.153.

Museum of Modern Art

11 West 53rd Street
708–9490

Constantly changing programmes in the Video Gallery. Free with museum admission (see p.116).

City nights:
Jazz clubs and dance palaces

'A civilized man never goes to bed on the same day he gets up' –
Jimmy Walker, Mayor of New York, 1925–32.

Jazz

The golden age of New York jazz was in the late 1940s and early
1950s: a creative explosion that crystallized around Charles Parker.
Some of the great names are still around, and some new ones have
arrived. Generally the first set begins at 9 or 9.30 p.m.; second set
at 11; extra sets on Friday and Saturday nights at 1 a.m. . . . but
this will vary from place to place. Expect a cover charge (anywhere
from $10 to $20) and/or a minimum for drinks. Most take American
Express/Mastercard (Access)/VISA; exceptions are noted below.

Best listings are in the *Voice*, *New York* and *Downbeat*. Or call the
Jazzline: 718–465–7500, 24 hours.

A sampling, and an idea of who might be playing where:

Blue Note

131 West 3rd Street (near Sixth Avenue)
475–8592

Recently resuscitated, with Sarah Vaughan, Carmen McRae, Oscar
Peterson, the MJQ, and their ilk. Music from 9.00 p.m., with after-
hours sets.

Bradley's

70 University Place (between 10th and 11th Streets)
228–6440

Cool, calm, and collected. At the restaurant tables in the back, steaks and other rather ordinary entrées are in the $11–$13 range. Sunday brunch, from noon to 4.00 p.m., is a fine time to check out local pianists – the set begins at 2.00 p.m.; nightly sets begin at 9.45.

Burgundy

467 Amsterdam (between 82nd and 83rd Streets)
787–8300

Substantial Upper West Side jazz. Jimmie Ponder. . .

Cafe Carlyle

35 East 76th Street (between Fifth and Madison Avenues)

Bobby Short plays Cole Porter, Gershwin, Rogers and Hart at the Carlyle, Tuesday to Saturday at 10.00 p.m. and midnight. Cover is $20 ($25 on Friday and Saturday); no minimum, but you're not likely to sit at a table without a glass of something. An expensive treat. Dress up.

Carnegie Tavern

165 West 56th Street
757–9522

Another musicians' stomping ground. Ellis Larkin . . .

Fat Tuesday's

190 Third Avenue (at 17th Street)
533–7902

Stan Getz, Astrud Gilberto, Les Paul, Mose Allison . . .

Lush Life

184 Thompson Street (at Bleecker Street)
228–3788

Ahmad Jamal, Toshiko Akiyoshi, Philly Joe Jones . . .

One Fifth Avenue

1 Fifth Avenue (at 8th Street)
260–3434

A pricey, trendy bar, specializing in young vocalists and pianists.
Elegant early Cunard decor and a spiffy young clientele.

Sweet Basil

88 Seventh Avenue South (at Bleecker Street)
242–1785

Small, crowded, and prone to invite big bands. Pharaoh Sanders,
Gil Evans, Sun Ra, Art Blakey . . .

Village Gate

Bleecker and Thompson Streets
255–4037

Big bands downstairs, combos on the Terrace. Heavy duty Latin
music: Tito Puente and his ilk. No credit cards.

Village Vanguard

178 Seventh Avenue South (at 11th Street)
255–4037

A large, low, intimate room, dear to the hearts of aficionados. Milt
Jackson, Art Farmer, Billy Higgins, Elvin Jones, Mel Lewis . . . No
credit cards.

West End

2911 Broadway (at 113th Street)
666–8750

A back-room Columbia University hangout: small groups, established and up-and-coming musicians. Chico Hamilton, Clark Terry, Ray Barretto . . .

Street music

Washington Square on weekends, if you can stand the company.

Columbus Avenue in the sixties and seventies, for occasionally excellent lone sax players.

Grand Army Plaza (59th Street and Fifth Avenue) for good bands trying to make themselves heard above the traffic.

Central Park on sunny Sundays – there seem to be hundreds of little combos, ranging from Dixieland to progressive, clustered around the statuary in the lower reaches of the park. Contributions appreciated.

Eclectic

Apollo Theater

253 West 125th Street (between Seventh and Eighth Avenues)
749–5838

You're in luck. After mouldering as a movie house for years, the Apollo Theater has been resplendently renovated, and the first thing it did was to reinstate Wednesday Amateur Nights. If that doesn't make you run toward the subway, be advised that it was from the stage of Harlem's Apollo that Ella Fitzgerald, Sarah Vaughan, James Brown, the Jackson Five . . . Frankie Lyman and the Teen-agers! . . . got their starts. And the audience is as legendary as the acts.

Lone Star Cafe

Fifth Avenue (at 13th Street)
242–1664

This used to be a genteel soda fountain for the grandmother market; now it's a Texas-style saloon serving the best in country-and-western (and other) music. Curtis Mayfield, Commander Cody, Pure Prairie League . . .

Folk City

130 West 3rd Street
254–8449

Primeval. Bob Dylan croaked his first few stanzas here. Currently: Livingston Taylor and lesser lights. No credit cards.

Dancing

Places to be seen, or to fade into the crowd. Ballroom – metal – salsa – disco – reggae. Cover ranges from $5 to $20, and with one exception nothing begins to happen before 9.30 or 10.00 p.m.

Area

157 Hudson Street (south of Canal Street)
226–8423

Music, dance, and *props*. Crazy, rich and outrageous. The club is packed, and so are the sidewalks outside, with crowds waiting to get in. Every six weeks a new theme . . . but as the visuals become more outré, the sounds are more maintstream. $15 cover.

Corso

205 East 86th Street
534–4964

Salsa. Cover: $10 on weekends. On Wednesdays, Fridays, and Sundays, women admitted free till 11.00 p.m.

Danceteria

300 West 21st Street
620–0790

Young crowd. Cover: $8 before 11.00 p.m., $12 after.

Ethnic Folk Arts Center

179 Varick Street, upstairs
691–9510

Folk dancing: Balkan, Israeli and what-have-you. Lessons from
7.00 p.m. to 8.30 p.m., dancing till midnight. Live band the last
Friday of every month. $4.

Heartbreak

179 Varick Street
691–2388

Music of the '50s and '60s in the most appropriate setting imagin-
able. Live bands Mondays. $15.

Juke Box NYC

304 East 39th Street (at Second Avenue)
685–1556

Casual. $5 cover.

Limelight

47 West 20th Street
807–7850

A flashy young crowd crammed into an erstwhile church. Full of
odd alcoves. Cover: $15.

Pyramid Club

101 Avenue A (near 7th Street)
420–1590

Progressive music (a euphemism for punk?) and live bands. Sundays
are best. Cover: $10.

Red Parrot

617 West 57th Street
247–1530

A live orchestra plays sounds of 1940s and 1950s on Saturdays and Sundays. Cover: $15.

Reggae Lounge

285 West Broadway
226–4598

Heavy Jamaican reggae week-nights, and the more danceable stuff on weekends. The crowd consists of Rastafarians, Africans, Europeans, students. Cover: $10 on Saturdays, $6 for students.

Ritz

119 East 11th Street
254–2800

A rescued ballroom, with live bands playing everything from punk to jazz. Casual and populous. $10 Friday, $11 Saturday.

Roseland

239 West 52nd Street
247–0200

Sixty-five years old, cavernous and legendary. Big bands and Latin dancing Thursdays and Sundays, disco on Fridays. Dancing from 2.30 p.m. to midnight, and till 11.00 p.m. on Saturdays. Contests! Cover: $7 on Fridays, $10 on Saturdays, $8 on Sundays.

Roxy Roller Rink

515 West 18th Street
675–8300

Roller dancing, with a young black and Hispanic clientele, Sundays to Wednesdays, bebop on Fridays and Saturdays. Electrifying. Cover: $10.

Visage

610 West 56th Street
247–0612

Another place to see and be seen. Velvet walls, American Realist sculpture, Lalique crystal masks. Plus a pool, and ice shows. $15 cover.

City sights:
Parks, relics and obsessions

The parks

With one profound exception, New York plays its green space close to the chest. Some of its most delightful parks and gardens are hidden in unlikely corners, or sprinkled parsimoniously along the boulevards: the strip of green that divides traffic along Park Avenue would make a decent bit of acreage, lumped together. There are minute 'vest pocket' parks between midtown buildings, and plenty of glassed-in atriums in corporate headquarters. There are neighbourhood squares that consist of a statue, a playground and a few sprigs of grass between the cobbles. There are lonely wildwood parks that invite no one but muggers and their prey. And there is Central Park.

Central Park

It's not just geographically central – it actually shaped the city's spirit. Designed in 1857, it inspired the 'City Beautiful' movement of the 1870s, the fount of everything magnificent about New York; and it's a democratic free-zone in the heart of the city, explored and adored by all. Like everything else in the city, it's pure artifice, even though its designers, Frederick Law Olmsted and Calvert Vaux, intended it as a rural refuge for city-dwellers. The variety of landscape is astonishing: a tranquil, reflecting pond in the southeast corner, magical at dusk; the vast, pastoral Sheep Meadow (now sheepless); a maze of wooded paths through the Ramble in mid-park; the washed-out brick and sandstone elegance of the Bethesda Fountain;

an immaculate Conservatory Garden on the northeast edge; and the wilderness of the northern territories of the park. Scattered throughout are rugged outcroppings of bedrock – Manhattan schist – and there is water everywhere: formal ponds, placid lakes and (drought permitting) occasional brooks. There are American elms along the Mall, and black cherries everywhere; hawthorns and dogwoods; lilacs east of the Sheep Meadow; horse chestnuts along the drives; and flowering cherry trees west of the Reservoir.

Central Park on the first good day of the year: clumsy rowboats on the Lake; jazz bands bunched around every statue; roller skaters in shorts and earphones; model yachts in the Conservatory Pond – everything from clipper ships to submarines to robot rowers. Softball and soccer in the playing fields of the Lawn; multitudes of suntanners. The ritual reading of the *Sunday Times* takes place in rowboats and on park benches. Old-timers play bocce on a manicured pitch; children clamber all over Alice's bronze mushroom; displaced Poles circle around the Poland statue, muttering. Hot dogs . . . ice cream . . . soda. The Israel Day parade blares down Fifth Avenue, echoes penetrating the park: Hava Nagila on bagpipes. The Melting Pot revisited.

Central Park provides about the only recreational facilities New Yorkers ever know. Most are open from 8 a.m. to dusk. The roads that intersect the park are off limits to cars (but swarming with runners and cyclists) from Friday evening to early Monday morning and from spring to fall during non-rush hours on weekdays. Horses can be rented from the Claremont Stables (175 West 89th Street, 724–5100) at $18 an hour . . . you'd be better off bringing your own. For boat and bike rental, there's the Loeb Boathouse on the Lake (near the East 72nd Street entrance): both about $4 an hour. Ice skating in the Wollman Memorial Rink (East 60th Street entrance) is indefinitely on hold: if it ever reopens, it's cheaper and less conspicuous (for those whose ankles buckle) than in the public glare of the Rockefeller Center rink. There are public tennis courts near West 93rd Street; squash and handball courts at North Meadow Recreation Center (East or West 97th Street entrances); bocce and croquet lawns north of the Sheep Meadow; and basketball courts northeast of the Great Lawn. The Carousel west of the Dairy (East 65th Street entrance) is no antique, but not to be scorned; and there are more than twenty playgrounds for children.

For less active pursuits, or just for refuge from the city's clamour:

Battery Park

Battery Place and State Street

Herman Melville's water-gazers still keep an eye on the harbour, the Statue of Liberty, the Staten Island Ferry and (rarely now) the freighters and liners that dock in New York. The park is cluttered with war memorials, and there's not much greenery, but the air is fresh and washed, and the outward view is sweeping.

Bowling Green

Broadway at Beaver Street

New York's first public park – a minuscule 18th-century pitch for lawn bowling. The iron fence is original – 1771 – but its caps were knocked off within five years in an excess of revolutionary zeal.

Brooklyn Botanic Garden

Prospect Park, Brooklyn
622–4433

Hours: Tuesday–Friday, 8.00 a.m.–6.00 p.m. Saturdays, Sundays, Holidays: 10.00 a.m.–6.00 p.m. (Closes at 4.30 p.m., 1 October–31 March)
Admission free

Transport: Seventh Avenue IRT Express, nos. 2 or 3, to Eastern Parkway. Fifty acres of exuberant plantings: rose gardens, a cherry esplanade, dogwoods (a spring delight), magnolias, a Japanese hill-and-pond garden, a reproduction of the Zen garden at Ryoanji, a fragrance garden (labelled in Braille), a Shakespeare garden, and a magnificent conservatory.

Bryant Park

42nd Street (between Fifth and Sixth Avenues)

The park behind the Library: neoclassical white marble filtered through green trees, very easy on the eye, and an excellent place to re-group after the rigours of midtown. The major recreational activities here are chess matches and drug hustling, but renovation is being attempted.

Carl Schurz Park

East 81st to 90th Street, along East End Avenue

The walkways surround Gracie Mansion, the Mayor's official residence, and worth noting on your way to the esplanade: this is known as John Finley Walk – invigorating in brisk weather – and looks out over the East River to the Triborough and Hell Gate bridges to the north and the 59th Street Bridge to the south. Between them: the borough of Queens.

Fort Tryon Park

Broadway to Riverside Drive
(between 192nd and Dyckman Streets)

A tangle of paved pathways high above the Hudson, romantically landscaped: lawns, rock gardens, terraces and little woodlands. The Cloisters, at the north end of the park – the Metropolitan Museum's repository for medieval art – are distinctly other-worldly.

Madison Square Park

23rd Street (between Fifth and Madison Avenues)

Neither large nor prepossessing, but adequate for sandwiches while you admire the majesty of the Flatiron Building.

Samuel Paley Plaza

3 East 53rd Street (between Fifth and Madison Avenues)

A vest-pocket park: paved, thoughtfully provided with iron lawn-furniture, honey-locust trees, and a soothing waterfall. Ideal for lunch if you can squeeze in among the office workers . . . at other times, a fine place to take the weight off your feet.

Prospect Park

Grand Army Plaza to Parkside Avenue, Brooklyn

An immense palette for Olmsted & Vaux, the designers of Central Park. Curious quirks are scattered among the terraces and gardens: a miniature Zoo with WPA (i.e. Depression-era) murals illustrating Kipling; a Bamboo Grove; four or five Triumphal Arches; a Boulder Bridge; an Italianate Boathouse; a Croquet Shelter; an Oriental Pavilion; and, at the Park Circle entrance, Heroic Equestrian Sculpture.

Riverside Park

From 72nd to 158th Streets, west of Riverside Drive

Yet another Olmsted & Vaux triumph: a rolling rivulet of a park, running in tandem with the Hudson, neglected by almost everyone. One of its mysteries is a walled circular fountain near the entrance to the 79th Street Marina, part of a complex traffic distribution system. The outcropping at 84th Street, known as Mount Tom, was one of Poe's favourite brooding-grounds. Northward, the bronze and marble statuary is thick on the ground.

Union Square

Broadway and 14th Street

A marketplace for drugs until a year or so ago, when the city closed it down and remodelled it. Now it has reopened with new shrubs and flower beds, benches and drinking fountains, and glass and cast-iron kiosks at the subway entrances. On Saturdays, from spring to fall, a lively 'green market' springs up: fresh produce from New Jersey truck farms.

United Nations North Garden

U.N. Plaza (at 48th Street)

A tranquil sculpture garden, fanned by East River breezes, with donations by member-nations scattered among the lawns and shrubbery. Dignitaries come and go, talking of anything but Michelangelo.

Washington Square Park

South end of Fifth Avenue (between Waverly Place and West 4th Street)

If anyone's to blame for the degradation of this once-innocent and cheerful park, it's Bob Dylan, who popularized Bohemia. The flocks of folk-singers have been followed by several waves of punked-out disco freaks, equipped with industrial-strength radios and an assortment of pharmaceuticals, and the park is now unfit for human habitation.

Relics and obsessions

For a city that's young by European standards, New York has an obsessive interest in its own past. There are reliquaries of just about everyone's history in tiny, specialized museums. And there are collections of art and artifacts that relate to almost every subject. Here are some of the major repositories, with a few curiosities mixed in.

Abigail Adams Smith Museum

421 East 61st Street
838–6878

Hours: Monday–Friday, 10.00 a.m.–4.00 p.m.
Admission: Adults, $2, Senior Citizens, $1,
Children under 12, free with adult

A 1799 carriage house converted into a residence in 1826, now preserved by the Colonial Dames of America. An incongruous little brick-and-stone farmhouse set in a tiny garden.

American Museum of Natural History

Central Park West between 77th and 81st Streets
873–1300

Hours: Monday, Tuesday, Thursday, Sunday,
10.00 a.m.–5.45 p.m. Wednesday, Friday, Saturday,
10.00 a.m.–9.00 p.m.
Admission: Adults $3, Children $1.50
Free after 5.00 p.m. on Fridays and Saturdays
Subway: From the East Side: Lexington Avenue IRT (no. 6) to
77th Street and M17 crosstown bus to Central Park West. From
the West Side: Eighth Avenue IND (AA or CC) to 81st Street.

Teddy Roosevelt's stupendous monument: cavernous exhibitions,
dusty dioramas, elaborate reconstructions of the world's wilder-
nesses. Halls of African Mammals, Ocean Life, Asian Peoples,
Indians and Eastern Woodlands, and much, much more. Check
out the dinosaurs, the 94-foot whale, the Star of India sapphire in
the Hall of Minerals. A telling note: on days when the city's public
schools are in session, the Museum (and the Planetarium) don't
admit people under 18 before 2.00 p.m. without an adult in tow.

Black Fashion Museum

155–57 West 126th Street
666–1320

Hours: Monday–Friday, 12.00 p.m.–8.00 p.m. (by appointment)
Admission: Donation

Special shows: national costumes of Third World ambassadors, or
day-clothes of black American businesswomen, for example.

Brooklyn Children's Museum

145 Brooklyn Avenue (corner of St Marks and Brooklyn Avenues)
718–735–4432

Hours: Monday, Wednesday, Thursday, Friday,
1.00 p.m.–5.00 p.m. Saturday, Sunday, school holidays,
10.00 a.m.–5.00 p.m.
Transport: Seventh Avenue IRT (No. 3) to Kingston Avenue.

Walk one block west to Brooklyn Avenue, six blocks north to the Museum.
Eighth Avenue IND (A) to Kingston-Throop Avenue. Walk one block west to Brooklyn Avenue, six blocks south to the Museum.

The world's first children's museum – established in 1889. Hundreds of events and activities. Hands-on exhibits and participatory programmes. Innumerable cultural and natural history artefacts.

City Hall

Broadway at Murray Street

Open Monday–Friday, 10.00 a.m.–3.30 p.m.

Early nineteenth-century French renaissance, housing the City Council, the Board of Estimate, and the Mayor's office: after Koch (who will still be Mayor decades from now) the deluge. The Governor's Room houses fine political portraits by Sully, Inman, Trumbull, et al.

Dog Museum of America

51 Madison Avenue (at 27th Street)
696–8350

Hours: Tuesday–Saturday, 10.00 a.m.–5.00 p.m. Wednesday, 10.00 a.m.–7.00 p.m.

If you've finally run out of things to do in New York, this is for you.

Ellis Island

April–October
Transport: Circle Line ferry from Battery Park (South Ferry subway station). Schedule: 269–5755.
Guided tour by the National Park Service: Adults, $2, Children under 12, $1

The former immigration station, through which the parents and grandparents of millions of Americans passed. Cavernous, spooky, and still full of ancestral hopes and fears.

Empire State Building

5th Avenue (at 34th Street)

Observation Deck hours: Monday-Sunday, 9.30 a.m. to midnight
Adults, $3; Senior Citizens, $2; Children, $1.75

Since it was humbled by the Sears Tower in Chicago and the World
Trade Center in lower Manhattan, the Empire State has come down
in the world. But for an unparalleled view of *midtown* Manhattan it's
still the best. The corridors of the ground floor are slightly eery:
elaborate marble-and-steel, black-and-silver deco: like walking
through a 'thirties movie. Observation Decks on the 86th and 102nd
floors.

Fashion Institute of Technology

227 West 27th Street (between Seventh and Eighth Avenues)
Gallery information: 760–7760

Hours: Tuesday 10.00 a.m.–9.00 p.m. Wednesday–Saturday
10.00 a.m.–5.00 p.m.
Admission: Free

New York's school for future fashion designers – has several exhibitions going at any time: textiles, clothes, accessories. Inquire at the
Shirley Goodman Resource Center. Some shows require admission
charges.

Fire Department Museum

104 Duane Street (near Broadway)
570–4230

Hours: Monday–Friday, 9.00 a.m.–4.00 p.m.
Admission: Free
Antique fire engines and fire department history.

Grant's Tomb

Riverside Drive at 122nd Street
666–1640

Hours: Wednesday–Sunday, 9.00 a.m.–5.00 p.m. Admission: Free

No one we know has ever visited Grant's Tomb. Reputedly it offers historical information on the life and times of the ex-Union general-turned-president. You can be the first to find out.

Hayden Planetarium

Central Park West (at 81st Street)
873–8828

Hours: Monday–Friday, noon–4.45 p.m. Saturday,
10.00 a.m.–5.00 p.m. Sunday noon–5.45 p.m. (October–June);
Saturday, noon–5.45 p.m. Sunday, noon–4.45 p.m.
(July–September)

Part of the Museum of Natural History. A guided tour of the universe.

Japan House Gallery

333 East 47th Street
832–1155

Hours: Tuesday–Sunday 11.00 a.m.–5.00 p.m.
Admission: Donation

Three major shows of Japanese arts and crafts annually: a collection of warlord helmets, for example. Second floor of Japan House. Always the height of elegance.

Museo del Barrio

1230 Fifth Avenue
831–7272

Hours: Tuesday–Friday, 10.30 a.m.–4.30 p.m. Saturday–Sunday,
11.00 a.m.–4.00 p.m.

Admission: Donation

The art and culture of Latin America and Puerto Rico – located on the edge of Spanish Harlem.

Museum of the American Indian

Audubon Terrace (Broadway and West 155th Street)
283–2420

Hours: Tuesday–Saturday, 10.00 a.m.–5.00 p.m. Sunday,
1.00 p.m.–5.00 p.m.
Admission: Adults, $2, Students/Senior Citizens, $1

Immense collection of native American art and artifacts from Tierra
del Fuego to Alaska.

Museum of Broadcasting

1 East 53rd Street (just east of Fifth Avenue)
752–7684

Hours: Wednesday–Saturday: noon–5.00 p.m.; Tuesday:
noon–8.00 p.m.
Admission: General, $3; Students, $2; Children under 13/Senior
Citizens, $1.50.

No artefacts, but an immense collection of broadcast programmes:
Roosevelt's Fireside Chats, Edward R. Murrow's 'This . . . is
London' World War II broadcasts, and the whole gamut of American radio entertainment. Television shows from TV's 'golden age'
through the Watergate hearings to the present. Visitors can use the
Museum's radio/TV consoles for an hour at a time. There are also
daily special-interest programmes in the Museum's theatre and
videotheques – retrospectives of a television performer or director,
for example – and a library of 2,400 rare radio production scripts.
It's a goldmine for buffs and dilettantes alike.

Museum of the City of New York

1220 Fifth Avenue (at 103rd Street)
534–1672

Hours: Tuesday–Saturday,   10.00 a.m.–5.00 p.m.   Sunday,
1.00 p.m.–5.00 p.m.
Admission: Free

The ethnic face of New York.

Museum of Holography

11 Mercer Street
925–0526

Hours: Wednesday–Sunday, noon–6.00 p.m.
Admission: Adults, $2.75; Children under 12/Senior Citizens,
$1.50

An old cast-iron building in SoHo full of three-dimensional
photography – invented in 1947 by a Hungarian physicist. The
Museum is the world's biggest (perhaps only) repository of information on the subject: plenty of exhibitions and demos.

New York Children's Museum

314 West 54th Street
765–5904

Hours: Wednesday–Sunday, 1 p.m.–5 p.m. Children: $2 ($3 on
weekends and holidays), Adults: $1 ($2 on weekends and holidays);

Participatory exhibitions, books, games, toys, and arts-and-crafts
classes.

New York Historical Society

170 Central Park West (between 76th and 77th Streets)

Hours: Tuesday–Friday, 11.00 a.m.–5.00 p.m. Saturday,
10.00 a.m.–5.00 p.m. Sunday, 1.00 p.m.–5.00 p.m. Closed
Monday
Admission: General, $2; Children, 75¢
Information: 873–3400

New York's oldest museum – founded in 1804. An astounding
collection of fire engines and carriages in the basement; hundreds of
Audubon watercolours on the fourth floor; portraits and landscapes,
fashion plates, furniture, photographs, Tiffany lamps and other
memorabilia of the city scattered throughout. And the temporary
exhibitions are always fascinating.

New York Public Library

Fifth Avenue at 42nd Street
221–7676

Central Research Library exhibtions
Hours: Monday–Wednesday, 10.00 a.m.–9.00 p.m.
Thursday–Saturday, 10.00 a.m.–6.00 p.m.

The marble Library Lions guarding the entrance are every New
Yorker's sentimental favourites. The neo-classical building itself is
a masterpiece. Free tours depart from the lobby, Mondays to Saturdays, at 11.00 a.m. and 2.00 p.m.

Library exhibitions are held in the Gottesman Exhibition Hall:
rare books, prints and manuscripts on a theme (censorship was a
big one in 1985). Other exhibits can occasionally be found in the
second-floor hallways.

If you're visiting the library for purposes other than touristic,
take the stairs (marble, beautiful) to the public catalogue and main
reading rooms on the third floor. Check the card catalogues and
bound indexes for the book you want, fill out a call slip and file it
at the information desk in the public catalogue room. Eventually
the book is brought to that desk – you're notified by indicator board
overhead. The book can be used only in the reading room, but you
can spend all day there. A rewarding spot, immense and stately,
even without something to read.

The Annex, 521 West 43rd Street, contains copies of more than
4000 newspapers published all over the world since 1800. Plus
bound files and microform copies of all US patents since 1872.
Open Monday–Saturday, 9.00 a.m.–5.00 p.m.

'Old Merchant's House'

29 East 4th Street (between Lafayette Street and the Bowery)
777–1089

Admission: General, $2; Students/Senior Citizens, $1.

A beautifully restored Federal row-house, the last one left on this
East Village block. Open by appointment. Across the street there's
an odd little gallery that sells oxidized copper objets d'art.

Police Academy Museum

235 East 20th Street
477–9753

Hours: Monday-Friday, 9.00 a.m.–3.00 p.m.
Admission: Free

Nostalgia for law-enforcement aficionados.

Schomburg Center

515 Lenox Avenue (at 135th Street)
862–4000

Hours: Monday/Wednesday, noon–8.00 p.m. Tuesday/Thursday/
Friday, 10.00 a.m.–6.00 p.m.

Admission: Free
Black history and art, from earliest Africa to latest Harlem.

South Street Seaport Museum

16 Fulton Street (at the East River)
766–9020

Hours: Monday–Saturday, 10.00 a.m.–8.00 p.m. Sunday,
10.00 a.m.–6.00 p.m. Ships close at 6.00 p.m.; piers close at dusk
Admission: Adults, $3.50, Children, $1.50

Lower Manhattan's nautical history, on the former site of the Fulton
Fish Market: restored streets, square riggers, the sailors' dives of
Water Street. Numerous tours and activities: you can even cruise
the harbour for a couple of hours on the schooner *Pioneer*. And free
jazz concerts on Pier 16 in summer. Drawback: everyone you see
will be a tourist or a concessionaire.

Ukrainian Museum

203 Second Avenue (at 12th Street)
228–0110

Hours: Wednesday–Sunday, 1.00 p.m.–5.00 p.m.
Admission: Adults, $1
Students/Senior Citizens, 50¢

Folk art and neighbourhood roots: costumes, Russian Easter eggs, photo exhibits.

Coach tours

There are scores of coach tours of the city and environs: they'll cost you anywhere from $8 for a couple of hours to $25 for an all-day excursion; they can take in the whole town or focus on a specific neighbourhood. (My feeling is that you'll see more as a pedestrian.) The heavy-duty coach firms are:

Gray Line

900 Eighth Avenue (at 54th Street)
397–2600

Short Line

166 West 46th Street
354–5122

Boat rides

Circle Line

Pier 83, Circle Line Plaza, west end of 42nd Street
563–3200

Dates: April to mid-November, Monday–Sunday
Hours: Variable with season; call for specifics
Cost: General, $10; Children under 12, $5

A three-hour, 35-mile, anticlockwise cruise around Manhattan. An excellent way to get some idea of the scale of the city, and worth it for the beauty of the bridges alone – the George Washington and Brooklyn Bridges, especially.

Hudson River Day Line

Pier 81, Circle Line Plaza, west end of 41st Street
279–5151

Dates: end of May to mid-September; Wednesday, Thursday,

Saturday, Sunday; Departure at 9.30 a.m.; return at 6.30 p.m.
Round-trip fares: Adults, $12, Senior Citizens, $10, Children under
12, $6
(One-way fares are about two-thirds of round trip.)

An all-day cruise up the Hudson to Bear Mountain State Park and
West Point (the US Military Academy, which you can tour for
another $3). The ship continues as far north as Poughkeepsie, but
turns around there without stopping. Along the way: the Palisades
of New Jersey; Sing Sing prison; High Tor; Storm King Mountain.
A pleasant perusal of the Hudson River landscape. Cafeteria, bar
and snack bars aboard.

Walking tours

The only ones I'd recommend are the non-profit variety. For the
guides, it's generally a labour of love.

New York City Public History Project

445 West 59th Street, NYC 10019
489–3566

Cost: Free

On-the-spot histories of urban housing (in the East Village),
financial gymnastics (Wall Street), and other facets of city life as
they were and are. A limit of 25 per tour, so call well in advance.

Friends of Cast Iron Architecture

369–6004

The Friends no longer escort pedestrians around SoHo, but they've
published an excellent do-it-yourself pamphlet ($2.50 from Urban
Center Books, located in the north wing of the Palace Hotel,
Madison Avenue and 51st Street): the history and relics (mostly on
Broome Street) of this distinctively late 19th century New York
architectural technique.

Friends of Central Park

16 East 8th Street
473–6283

Cost: $1 contribution toward park restoration.
Dates: May–October

Very informal visits to the wilds of Central Park; and the Friends
can give you a line on walking tours of some out-of-the-way parks
in the boroughs and beyond. Previous excursions have gone to the
Valentine Varian House in the Bronx; the BAM Park and the
Wyckoff House, in Brooklyn; the Lockwood-Mathews Mansion in
Norwalk, Connecticut . . . one group of cyclists met at the
Guggenheim Museum at 2.30 a.m. and headed for a sunrise break-
fast at the Battery.

Sunday Walking Tours

Museum of the City of New York
Fifth Avenue at 103rd Street, NYC 10029
534–1672

Cost: $6
March–October, rain or shine

Tours depart at 1.30 p.m. from neighbourhood landmarks.
Leisurely strolls through a variety of districts, led by the Museum's
experts: Park Slope and Brooklyn Heights; Astor Place, Greenwich
Village and SoHo; Madison Square, Gramercy Park, Chelsea and
much more. This is one of the best ways I know to catch up on the
historical and architectural details of the city.

92nd Street Y Tours

1395 Lexington Avenue
831–8603

Walking tours of city districts; 'activity' tours – like mushroom
hunting on Staten Island; bus tours out of town; artists' studio and
auction house tours. Anywhere from $8 for a local perambulation
to $55 for an extended excursion.

Indoor Tours
Metropolitan Opera House Backstage Tours

c/o Education at the Met
1865 Broadway, NYC 10023
582–3512

Dates: October–June; Weekdays: 3.45 p.m. Saturdays: 10.30 a.m.
Cost: General, $5; Students, $3

Advance reservations required; call or write.
Costumes, sets, wigs, rehearsal halls, dressing rooms, the stage and
the auditorium: all the processes involved in producing an opera.

Radio City Music Hall Backstage Tours

1260 Sixth Avenue (at 50th Street)
757–3100

Hours: noon–4.45 p.m., approximately on the hour, except on
special event days.
Cost: $3.95

Seven days a week, no reservations required to see this most deluxe
of the great Deco theatres.

Cemeteries

Probably not for the young at heart – and the big ones are not
particularly accessible. But if you're determined to be morbid:

Woodlawn Cemetery

Jerome and Bainbridge Avenue, Bronx

This is where you'll find Diana Barrymore, Vernon Castle, Duke
Ellington, Victor Herbert, Fiorello LaGuardia, R. H. Macy, Bat
Masterson, Herman Melville, Joseph Pulitzer, F. W. Woolworth,
and many, many more. Take the Lexington Avenue IRT (no. 4)
to Woodlawn – the end of the line, appropriately.

St John's Cemetery

801 Metropolitan Avenue, Queens
Near Forest Hills

This one – though it's in the borough of Queens – is operated by the Roman Catholic diocese of Brooklyn and it contains Charles 'Lucky' Luciano (1897–1962), Vito Genovese (1897–1969), Joseph Profaci (1897–1962) and Carlo Gambino (1902–76). All died of natural causes. The nearest subway stop is Metropolitan Avenue, Queens (via the BMT 'M' train); then it's a hefty walk up Metropolitan Avenue to the cemetery entrance.

Trinity Cemetery

Riverside Drive to Amsterdam Avenue,
West 153rd Street to West 155th Street
Opened only by arrangement with Trinity Parish, 602–0836.

This used to be part of John James Audubon's farm; it now houses (among others) Clement Clarke Moore, who wrote ''Twas the night before Christmas . . .' It's the only 'active' cemetery in Manhattan.

Trinity Church Cemetery

Wall Street and Broadway

Venerable. You'll find Alexander Hamilton and Robert Fulton here, as well as hordes of extant office workers, who use this little plot as a park.

Events

New York is not dull.

Parades

Parades are New York's answer to the blues. Every ethnic and national minority has its annual trip along Fifth Avenue, and a host of political, social and religious events are celebrated with brass bands, drum majorettes, banners, clowns, exotic millinery, outrageous costume and assorted monkeyshines. The best-attended and the most fun:

St Patrick's Day, 17 March, Fifth Avenue from 44th to 86th Street, then over to Third Avenue.

The Easter Parade, Fifth Avenue from St Patrick's Cathedral on 49th Street to 59th Street.

Brooklyn Bridge Day, second weekend in May, on the Bridge.

Martin Luther King, Jr, Memorial Day, 17 May, Fifth Avenue from 44th to 86th Street.

Steuben Day, third weekend in September, Fifth Avenue from 61st to 86th Street, then over to Third Avenue.

Pulaski Day, 4 October, Fifth Avenue from 28th to 52nd Street.

Columbus Day, 12 October, Fifth Avenue from 44th to 86th Street.

Halloween, 31 October, threading through the West Village and culminating in a blow-out in Washington Square.

Macy's Thanskgiving Day Parade, last Thursday in November, from 77th Street and Central Park West to Columbus Circle, then down Broadway to Herald Square.

For specifics on times and routes, call 397–8222.

Festivals

Festivals, street fairs and seasonal events are rife. You can't cross town without stumbling on some obscure celebration. Here is a sampling, without attempt at classification:

Chinese New Year, last week in January, on Mott Street, complete with dragon dances, fireworks and a mini-parade.

Hans Christian Andersen's Birthday, at his statue in Central Park, 2 April. Storytelling.

Egg-rolling Contest on the Great Lawn in Central Park, the Saturday before Easter. For children from five to thirteen, if they can stand the crush.

Gramercy Park Flower Show, last weekend in April, on the south side of the square.

St Joseph's Street Fair, last Saturday in May, at St Joseph's Church, Sixth Avenue and Washington Place.

Washington Square Outdoor Art Show, late May–early June and the last weekend in August and again in early September. The passers-by generally make better viewing than what's on display.

Kool Jazz Festival, the ten days preceding 4 July, takes place all over town. Call 787–2020 for information.

Fourth of July Fireworks, throughout New York Harbor. Riverside Park is the best vantage.

Japanese Obon Dance, the Saturday closest to 15 July, at Riverside Mall, 103rd Street and Riverside Drive.

Flatbush Frolic, second weekend in September, Cortelyou Road in Brooklyn. A neighbourhood shindig.

New York Is Book Country, third Sunday in September, Fifth Avenue from 47th to 57th Street. Words, words, words.

Atlantic Antic, third Sunday in September, a Middle Eastern festival on Atlantic Avenue in Brooklyn.

Tree-lighting ceremony at Rockefeller Center, early December.

Santa Lucia Day, 13 December, throughout Little Italy.

New Year's Eve in Times Square.

For information on most events, call 755–4100. And for the some of the edible aspects of New York street-fairs, see Festival Food, p.105.

Spectator sports

Madison Square Garden
From 31st to 33rd Street, between Seventh and Eighth Avenues
564–4400

This is the fourth Garden (three forerunners have burnt or been demolished) and the least lovable, but if you can't stay away from indoor spectator sports, it's Mecca. New York's home teams are the Knicks (basketball) and the Rangers (ice hockey), and both hold court at MSG from October to April. It's also the place to see world-class boxing, professional 'wrestling' (not exactly a sport), jai alai, rodeo, the circus . . . you name it.

Baseball, the national pastime, may look like nothing more than a gussied-up version of rounders, but it's actually subtle, complex and absorbing, and you'll never understand Americans until you've seen at least one game. New York has two 'major league' teams: the **Yankees**, possessors of a well-earned patrician hauteur, play at Yankee Stadium, in the South Bronx (293–6000); the **Mets**, upstarts making their way in the world, play at Shea Stadium in Queens (507–8499). Bleacher seats are the cheapest – as low as $4.50. Baseball season runs from April to October.

American football, which evolved (one assumes) from rugby, will make absolutely no sense to you if you don't have a firm grasp of the rules. The amount of time spent in actual play is about a tenth of that spent regrouping and reshuffling the players, but occasionally you'll see mind-boggling athletic feats and bombshell bursts of energy. The **New York Giants** play at Giant Stadium, in Rutherford, New Jersey (201–935–8500), and the **Jets** play at Shea Stadium, in Queens (421–6600). The season is from September to January.

Horseracing goes on at **Aqueduct**, in Queens (October to April), and **Belmont Park**, in Belmont, Long Island (May to October). Both are flat tracks, and Belmont is the site of the final event in the Triple Crown, the Belmont Stakes. For post times at both tracks, call the New York Racing Association, 641–4700. The harness tracks are at **Roosevelt Raceway**, in Westbury, Long Island (516–222–2000), and **Yonkers**, just north of the Bronx (914–968–4200). If you prefer to do your betting at a distance, try OTB (Off-Track Betting), the government's solution to illegal bookmaking. The old marble-shelved ticket windows in Grand Central Terminal are a picturesque place to place your bets, but there are plenty of other OTB outlets around town. Call 221–5624 for information.

For stay-at-homes there's plenty of live action in **Central Park:** model sailboat races on sunny days at the Conservatory Pond; amateur softball (a leisurely version of baseball) in the Hecksher Diamond and soccer matches on the Great Lawn; there are rumoured to be a cricket club and a rugby team somewhere in the vicinity; and if all else fails, you can watch the joggers sweating off the pounds at all hours of the day (but not at night; you don't belong here after dusk).

For a line on current sports information, call 976–1313.

Shopping

If you're a pauper in New York, you'd better face up to the fact that most of the shopping you do will be of the window variety. There's nothing you can't buy here, but if you have to translate pounds into dollars at current exchange rates, you'll probably discover that there's nothing on display that you absolutely have to have. If you can content yourself with just looking, read on.

The grand emporiums are Macy's (34th Street and Seventh Avenue) and Bloomingdale's (59th Street and Lexington Avenue). For sheer mass – for absolutely everything from shoelaces to pianos – Macy's is unparalleled. It's also refreshingly unpretentious: solid, brand-name merchandise sold at relatively modest prices; the drawback is the staggering rudeness of the staff. This is a store in which you're lucky to be ignored. Bloomingdale's is similarly cursed with a surly staff, and it has the added misfortune of a clientele whose grasp exceeds its reach: would-be patricians. What Bloomingdale's does best is display: everything from cosmetics to bedroom furniture is set off with up-to-the-minute laser technology, brilliant highlights, dramatic backdrops, outlandish props. Bloomingdale's is always on some kick: every six months, the whole place seems to be turned inside out and put back together with a new fashion statement.

The venues for serious perusal of clothes (women's division) are Henri Bendel, Bergdorf Goodman, Bonwit Teller: all in the nexus of 57th Street and Fifth Avenue. Each is relatively small and excruciatingly elegant, and everything is priced somewhere in outer space. Saks (at 50th Street and Fifth Avenue), Lord & Taylor (38th and Fifth) and the wonderful, respectable B. Altman (34th and Fifth) look positively bourgeois by comparison.

The smaller shops for women are naturally more daring than

these dowagers, and some of them dart in and out of fashion at a moment's notice. Some current favourites:

Betsey Johnson

248 Columbus Avenue (between 71st and 72nd Streets)

In the fall of 1985, *manic* was the word for her clothes.

Charivari Sport

2345 Broadway (at 85th Street)

and

Charivari Women

2307 Broadway (at 84th Street)

An outlet for Kenzo, and lesser breeds within the law. Sets the pace in New York – Charivari seems to outfit the entire Upper West side. Watch for August pre-inventory clearance sale.

Joseph Tricot

804 Madison Avenue

Austerity and elegance: pin-striped mid-calf skirts in black wool, with long, bulky, cream-coloured cardigans.

The area around **Spring Street** and **West Broadway**, in SoHo, is jammed with new-wave fashion joints: Dianne B., Victoria Falls, Fuel Injection, Morgan le Fey . . . clothes that require plenty of cash and more than a little chutzpah to get into.

On Madison Avenue, between 44th and 46th Streets, you'll find the five best men's clothing stores in the city: Brooks Brothers, F. R. Tripler, Paul Stuart, J. Press, and Chipp. Of these, the only one in which any noticeable change in style has occurred in the last twenty years is Paul Stuart. For up-tempo clothes, look into:

Madonna

223 East 60th Street (between Lexington and Third Avenues)

Pastel extremism

Charivari Sport

2345 Broadway (north side of 85th Street)

and

Charivari Men

2339 Broadway (south side of 85th Street)

Variations on a theme of excessive drape; runs the spectrum from black to grey.

Daval

82nd Street and Amsterdam Avenue.

Unbeatable for trend-setting socks, shorts, T-shirts and other non-durable goods; a small stock of jeans and jackets.

Discounts

Discount, gently used and retro clothes do exist in New York, and if you're hell-bent on buying them here instead of in London at half the price, be my guest.

Alice Underground

380 Columbus Avenue

Retro men's and women's clothes: white lace and bomber-jackets; slouch hats and wide ties.

Bolton's

Discount clothes for women, with scattered branches:
225 East 57th Street, between Seventh and Eighth Avenues
27 West 57th Street, off Fifth Avenue
1180 Madison Avenue
4 East 34th Street, off Fifth Avenue
etc., etc., etc.

Canal Jeans

304 Canal Street, at Broadway

Stocked to the rafters, at almost-wholesale prices.

Canal Surplus

363 Canal Street

Punk and war-zone material.

Civilian

164 Ninth Avenue, at 20th Street

Lavish fifties retro.

Encore

1132 Madison Avenue, between 85th and 86th Streets, upstairs

The best of the resale shops: two floors packed with racks of skirts, dresses, sweaters, coats, the works.

Eric

551 Third Avenue, between 76th and 77th Streets

Discount women's shoes.

The Finals

149 Mercer Street

Terrific swimwear at a discount.

Harriet Love

412 West Broadway, at Spring Street

Retro.

Hit or Miss

52 Duane Street

A TriBeCa outlet for discount women's clothes.

I. Michael

1041 Madison Avenue (between 79th and 80th Streets, upstairs)
A small selection of very nice, once-expensive women's clothes in good condition: $30–$150 for particularly fine items; excellent for conservative shirts and trousers.

NBO

1965 Broadway (at 68th Street)

Two enormous floors of discount men's clothes: shirts and slacks upstairs, suits and jackets in the basement.

P. L. Nimi

1323 Second Avenue (between 69th and 70th Streets)

Discount women's shoes

The New Store

289 Seventh Avenue (at 27th Street]

Discount women's clothes

Tri Shop

1689 1st Avenue (at 87th Street)

Discount women's clothes

Urban Outfitters

20 University Place (at 8th Street)

Discount men's clothes

Weiss & Mahoney

142 Fifth Avenue (at 19th Street)

The classic Army/Navy store, stuffed with jeans, camping equipment and military surplus.

Yuzen Kimono

318 East 6th Street

Vintage kimonos from the '30s to the '50s, $48–$66, in a tiny Lower East Side setting. Plus obis, wallets and other accoutrements from $10 to $20.

For true discount buffs – those who'd rather spend half an hour haggling than lose fifty cents on a deal – there's only one part of town of any interest: the Lower East Side, specifically Orchard Street and its surroundings. Sunday is the day to go – the whole area from Delaney to Houston Street is free of cars and packed with humanity well before noon. Just a few mentions to get you started:

Forman's

82 Orchard Street

Three floors of name-brand clothes, at least 20 per cent below department-store prices; everything on the third floor is 50 per cent off. Be prepared to plough through bales of stuff. A few doors up the street, at 92 Orchard, Forman's has a 'designer' branch, same discounts but pricier items.

Victory Shirt Co.

96 Orchard Street

Where else can you still get white-on-white shirts?

Rainbarrel

294 Grand Street

Women's overcoats and an abundance of raingear.

Flea markets

Flea markets are making a comeback. Try the one on 79th Street and Columbus Avenue, the IS-44 Market. It occurs on Sundays from about 11.00 a.m. onwards, a 'green market' for farmers' produce and much more; 'antiques' – i.e. deco artefacts from the 1930s, old clothes, junk of all descriptions; silverware, fiesta-ware, chemical glassware, costume jewellery, a huge selection of kimonos for between $10 and $25 – bright and dull, long and short, presided over by a feisty Japanese woman who's generally in some trouble over turf . . . And a few finger-food stands. Portobello Road in miniature. If this tantalizes you, you might also try the flea market in the PS-41 Playground, on Greenwich Avenue, north of 10th Street; but be advised that most of the faces, and at least half of the items on display, will be the same as those you saw uptown. For extreme funkiness, look into the two Saturday flea markets on Canal Street at Greene and Wooster Streets. While you're in the neighbourhood you might try (as I haven't dared) lunch in a diner at the top of Church Street called Exterminator Chilli.

For up-to-the-minute information on discounts and sales around town, the weekly *Sales and Bargains* column in *New York* magazine is a must. Leonore Fleischer has the world's best nose for cut-rate quality: not just clothes (though lots of clothes) but large and small home appliances, jewellery and accessories, textiles, cosmetics, furniture, potted plants, sports and exercise equipment, you name it.

Bookstores

New York has an abundance of bookstores, some of which can legitimately be called obscurantist.

Abbey Book Shop

61 Fourth Avenue (at 9th Street)

One of the last survivors in what used to be a paradise of second-hand bookstores.

Barnes & Noble

105 Fifth Avenue (at 18th Street)

Immense, crowded, and good value, but the help can be brusque and the checkout lines interminable. The only bookshop I know with a section entirely on Structuralism. Which may or may not be a virtue.

Barnes & Noble Sale Annex

128 Fifth Avenue (at 18th Street)

Discount books: 15 per cent off hard cover, 10 per cent off paperbacks, and 33 per cent off books on the *New York Times* bestseller list.

Complete Traveller

199 Madison Avenue (at 35th Street)

Travel books and maps – all corners of the globe, especially New York – served up by the friendliest possible staff.

Forbidden Planet

821 Broadway (at East 12th Street)

Science fiction, horror and comics from the 1930s to the present.

Foul Play

10 Eighth Avenue (at Bank Street)

An orderly mystery bookshop run by a woman who admits to enjoying the hard-boiled school but is versed in almost everything else.

Gotham Book Mart

41 West 47th Street

For rare and small press books: a classic bookstore.

Gryphon Books

2246 Broadway (at 81st Street)

For second-hand books and records, tiny and eclectic. Open seven days a week till midnight.

Murder Inc.

271 West 87th Street (between Broadway and Amsterdam Avenue)

Wry style, two cats and eclectic tastes. The shelves are stocked by genre: spy stories, Dutch *policiers*, hard-boiled California cops. Murder Inc. is now on an annual kick of giving horses to the New York Police Department in honour of Dick and Mary Francis.

New York Bound

43 West 54th Street

Everything there is to know about New York. Upstairs.

Oscar Wilde Memorial Bookshop

15 Christopher Street

A gay omnibus.

Shakespeare & Co.

2259 Broadway (at 81st Street)

General interest, excellent taste.

Soldier Shop

1222 Madison Avenue

War books and toy soldiers.

Strand Bookstore

828 Broadway (at 12th Street)

Immense and labyrinthine: more than two million used and out-of-print books. Review copies – the pristine pre-publication copies sent to the critics – are a speciality.

BOWLING-GREEN AND COMMENCEMENT OF BROADWAY.

Supersnipe

222 East 85th Street (between Second and Third Avenues)

Comics.

Womanbooks

201 West 92nd Street

A feminist bookstore.

Miscellany

A random sampling of unclassified curiosities:

Caswell-Massey

518 Lexington Avenue (at 48th Street)

A colonial pharmacy without pharmaceuticals: luxurious soaps and shaving gear, sachets, scents.

Crystal Resources

130–1/4 East 65th Street (off Lexington avenue)

Minerals and fossils; miraculous conglomerations of quartz.

Handblock

487 Columbus Avenue (at 83rd Street)

Folk-art fabrics from India and South America: made up into dresses, bedspreads, dish-towels and what-have-you, or sold by the yard.

Marimekko

7 West 56th Street

Alvar Aalto stools and vases, women's clothes, simple wooden toys, clear bold fabric, and other Finlandia.

Paprikas Weiss

1546 Second Avenue (between 82nd and 83rd Streets)

Kitchen gadgets, herbs and spices, Hungarian condiments and delicacies.

F.A.O. Schwarz

745 Fifth Avenue (at 58th Street) upstairs

From marbles to stuffed elephants to functional toy cars.

Sointu

20 East 69th Street (at Madison Avenue)

Everything small, everything superlatively designed, and almost everything in black or white. Household items, desk-top accessories, and jewellery refined almost out of existence.

Coping with New York

'Coping' is a native New York pastime: it means breaking even in your struggle to survive the city, and everyone has a personal bag of tricks with which to do so: odd bits of information, resources, suppliers, tactics and strategies that can free us all to spend time indulging in the city's pleasures, rather than dealing with its minor annoyances.

Animals

New Yorkers keep big dogs for protection and little ones for decoration. Some years ago, an enlightened administration made it mandatory for owners to clean up after their dogs, and the law is enforced. It's now possible to walk down the street with your head in the clouds and have no worries about what's underfoot. However, it does make one wonder how the dog-walking services (native to the Upper East Side) manage with their swirling packs of Afghans and whippets.

Cameras

Heavy-duty cameras are best left at home. They keep you from really seeing anything – you'll always be looking for photo opportunities, like a White House newshound. And they tab you as a tourist, an easy mark for the city's deft accessory-snatchers. If you must carry a camera, let it be a cheap little shooter that fits in your bag or pocket.

Children

If all else fails, take them to Coney Island. Or hire a sitter: many hotels maintain a list of local baby-sitters. Check when you arrive, or try one of the following services:

Avalon, 371–7222
Baby Sitters Association, 865–9348
Baby Sitters Guild, 682–0227
Gilbert Child Care Agency, 744–6770
Part Time Child Care Inc., 879–4343

Average cost is $5 per hour, with a four-hour minimum, plus $2 for daytime or $5 for evening transportation. The rates and conditions will vary with age of child and other considerations: in most cases the agency will want to know something about *you* before entrusting its sitters into your charge.

Other people's children, as you know, are an entirely different proposition from one's own. New York children, whether Park Avenue or Bed-Stuy, are without exception ill-mannered and out of control. Their behaviour problems seem to get worse on subways and buses. Ignore them and hope they'll go away.

Consulates

See under Emergencies, p.204.

Dial . . .

Dial-a-Hearing-Test: 737–4000
Dial-a-Joke: 976–3838
Dial-a-Prayer: 246–4200
Dial-a-Meditation-with-Sri-Chinmoy: 718–526–1111
Dial-a-Soap: 976–6363

Be advised that there's a 'service charge' for 976 numbers.

Electricity

American household current is a mild 110 volts, and it won't run British (or European) appliances unless they're dual-voltage. But look on the bright side: the only way you can electrocute yourself is by dropping a hair dryer into the tub, and even that isn't guaranteed.

Glossary

Bill (as in 'five-dollar bill') A note. But 'Send me the bill' means 'Invoice me by mail'. New Yorkers have as many terms for handling money as the eskimos have for snow; see below.
Break Can you (v.t.) break a twenty? Gimme a (n.) break, I'm (past participle) broke.
Chachkas Little objects that you schlepp around.
Check Cheque (in banks) or bill (in restaurants). 'If they'll take a check, I'll take care of the check'. And you can check in and out of hotels, check your luggage, check back with your agent. Street vendors importune you to 'check it out'.
Chutzpah Jewish hubris, or what it takes to live in New York.
Dates US 7/4/86 = UK 4/7/86.
Drugstore Chemist's, with extra added attractions: anything from a few packs of bobby-pins to a minor Woolworth's. A drugstore that sells prescription drugs is called a pharmacy.
Fall Autumn. The best time to be in New York.
First floor Ground floor. In hotels, the first floor is the Lobby; in department stores the second floor may well be the Mezzanine.
Garbage Rubbish. Dustmen are familiarly known as garbage men; in City Hall – which is rightly terrified of the garbage union – they're known as sanitation workers.
Glitzy Located somewhere in the fashion spectrum between glitter and kitsch.
Gridlock a traffic situation analogous to the stalemate in chess.
Hardware store Ironmonger's. For software, see Computerland.
Kvetch Complain.
Line Queue. People do line up in banks and at the movies, but for important things – subways and buses – the only British equivalent is the scrum.
Mail Post.

Nosh A bite to eat; used as a noun or as a verb, intransitively. Infinitely expandable: Noshateria; Nosharama; &c.

Or what? All-purpose emphasizer. 'Is this your idea of a joke, or what?' 'Are you going to get off the bus, or what?' Requires no reply, or a muttered one.

Person Euphemism for first person singular. 'A person could suffocate in this train.' 'That sort of talk could get back to a person.'

Phone booth Call box. Surprise: they work.

Rest room Public lavatory. See p.191.

Round trip Return ticket.

Schlepp To carry your chachkas all over town in a couple of shopping bags.

Schmattas Clothes, notably on Orchard Street in the Lower East Side.

Schmooze Chat.

Schnorrer Conniver.

Sleaze Times Square-itis.

Sidewalk Pavement. Possibly so named in New York because the only way you can get through the crowds is by walking sideways.

So A verbal shrug. 'So what's so bad?'

Subway Underground.

Tab Bill, in bars. If you run a tab, eventually you'll have to pick it up.

Underground Subversive.

Yiddish The lingua franca of New York.

Guide Books

Michelin Green Guide
Good maps, and excellent details and room plans of the major
museums.

A. I. A. Guide to New York City
Collier Books, New York. $13.95
White & Willensky are candidly in love with the city's architecture,
their city-lore is encyclopedic, and their prose is delightful.
Hundreds of photos, and superb maps with walking tours inked in.

500 Things to Do in New York for Free
New Century Publishers, New Jersey. $5.95
When this comprehensive catalogue came out, Sundays in New
York lost all excuse for dullness.

New York Art Guide
Art Guide Publications, London. £2.95
Thumbnail gallery, museum and miscellaneous-event reviews,
enough to give the more-than-casual buff an idea of what's going
on in the city. Published in London, and available at Zwemmer's.

The WPA Guide to New York City
Pantheon Books, New York. $8.95
Originally published by the Federal Writers' Project – a branch of
the New Deal – in the 1930s, and now reprinted. A view of New
York in time warp. One of my informants used the WPA Guide as
his sole source of information, no backup. Findings: the Plaza, listed
in the Guide at $7 a night, was even then the most expensive hotel
in town, and the Brooklyn Bridge is immutable, but many other
aspects of the city it describes have vanished or are sadly changed.
'Shortly before the Twentieth Century Limited leaves for Chicago
at six in the evening, a gray and red carpet is unrolled between the
gate and the platform.' Since then, both the carpet and the train
have disappeared.

Holidays

1 January; Memorial Day (last Monday in May); Independence Day (4 July); Labor Day (first Monday in September); Thanksgiving (last Thursday in November); Christmas. On religious holidays, Jewish businesses frequently remain open when secular ones close . . . and vice versa.

At certain times of the year there's no way to cross Fifth Avenue without disguising yourself as a drum majorette: Washington's Birthday (22 February), St Patrick's Day (17 March), Easter Sunday, Columbus Day (12 October). New Yorkers love a parade. See Events, p.168.

Information
New York Convention and Visitors' Bureau

2 Columbus Circle
397–8222

For basic tourist information, maps, brochures, and assistance.

Telephone information:

Directory Assistance for Manhattan and the other four boroughs: dial 411.
Elsewhere in the US and Canada: dial the Area Code + 555–1212. No charge if dialled from a pay phone.
Events information: 755–4100
Handicapped information: 566–3913
Jazzline 718–465–7500
Sportsphone: 976–1313
Time: 976–1616
Weather: 976–1212
Horoscope: a different number for each sign. Check the White Pages under Horoscopes-by-Phone.

Laundries and dry cleaners

Hotels will do your laundry for exorbitant fees (although one or two actually have coin-operated machines in the basement). There's no reason why you shouldn't hang a few drip-dryables in the shower, but be careful not to inconvenience the chambermaid. A nylon line from the shower-curtain rod to the shower-head will keep clothes from dripping on the floor, and a few clothes-pegs ('clothes pins' in the US) and a little detergent will make your portable laundry complete.

For non-drip items, there are laundromats (or 'laundramats' or 'laundermats') in likely locations around town: you're more liable to find one on Second Avenue, in the 20s, than on Fifth Avenue, in the 70s, obviously. Look under Laundries-Self-Service in the Yellow Pages for the nearest one. You'll need a plastic bag for haulage, and plenty of quarters. Almost as cheap, and much less hassle, is to find a 'service available' laundry: generally a laundromat with someone on duty who will wash and fold (but not iron) your clothes for about $4 for eight pounds. Drop them off in the morning and pick them up in the afternoon.

For non-do-it-yourself laundry, the city favours expensive French laundresses (Mme. Blanc, Mme. Renée, et al.) and the traditional Chinese, who mark your clothes in black ink. In either case, it'll take at least four days and plenty of cash to retrieve your clothes, but they do come back pressed and packaged.

There are about as many dry cleaners in town as there are lawyers, and some of them are very fast: the One Hour Martinizing chain, for instance. Location is an indication of cost: anything on the Upper East Side will set you back considerably more than the same service elsewhere.

Lavatories, public

They're called 'rest rooms' in the US and they're lamentably scarce. Sooner or later, you will find yourself frantically searching the concrete canyons for the nearest one – a miserable waste of time and effort which even veteran city-dwellers haven't solved for themselves. There are a number of ways to deal with this, listed in order of increasing desperation.

1 Head for public property:
City Hall
The Stock Exchange
Hospitals
Colleges and Universities
Train and bus stations (but not subways)
Department stores
The Library
The United Nations

2 Try the big hotels: the Plaza, the Pierre, the Waldorf. If it takes all your courage to walk through their portals, reflect on the importance of your mission, and remember that all big hotels have lots of public space: bars, restaurants, shops, lobbies; hence public WCs. The reward for courage is the extravagant decor of the loos.

3 Office buildings, especially the newest ones, try to stash their lavatories in odd corners, usually on the lower level if there is one. With persistence, you can find them. The RCA Building in Rockefeller Center is particularly coy in this regard.

4 Restaurants and coffee-shops will not let you use the WC unless you are at least a minimal patron. Likewise the museums.

Lifts

The unspoken rules for riding elevators are: face forward, fold hands in front of you, avoid eye contact, watch the numbers, and don't talk to anyone. New Yorkers won't get on an elevator offering less than two square feet per occupant. If you happen upon an empty elevator, it's good for a few knee bends or a loud scream on your way up (there's no place else in the city where you can do this: perfect privacy).

Lost and found

If you lose something on a bus or subway, there's a slim chance that it'll turn up in the Transit Authority's Lost Property Division, at 370 Jay Street, Brooklyn: 718–625–6200.

If you lose something in a cab, check with the Taxi & Limousine Commission's Lost Property Information department, 221 West 41st Street: 869–4513. Again, don't get your hopes up.

Manners

Everyone knows about the incivility of New Yorkers, but few realize that it's just a protective shell, and a fairly thin one, which you may be able to melt by turning on the charm. Asking directions, ordering lunch, trying on clothes, even waiting in line for the bus can be turned into a social exchange, and an opportunity for New Yorkers to display some rough-hewn charm of their own. But there will be times when you are treated with inexcusable rudeness. Options for dealing with it:

a Reply in kind. It won't help the situation, but a mild explosion may make you feel better.

b Ignore it. The easiest and emotionally cheapest way out.

c Repay it with extreme politeness – a subtle form of revenge. However: In Abraham & Strauss, a midtown department store, the *Times*'s Metropolitan Diarist overheard one shopper say, 'Excuse me,' to another, and the rebuff: 'If you want to be polite, go to Lord & Taylor.'

Maps

Flashmaps! New York is my favourite, because it's quick, concise and pocketable. It's $3.95 at bookstores.

Rand McNally and the AAA (American Automobile Association) put out excellent table-sized maps of New York, which are useful if you're spending time in the Boroughs, but don't ever try to open one up on a subway.

Media

Television may have been a British invention, but no one uses it so brilliantly for such ill ends as the Americans. If you find yourself in front of a tube with time to kill, here's what to watch for:

1 Commercials. 60-second brush-ups on American pop culture. Exorbitantly produced – far more so than the shows they support.

2 Trash. The morning game shows and afternoon soaps. If you can endure half an hour of these, you'll have instant insight into what the network moguls conceive of as the American housewife's psyche.

3 Saturday Night Live. 11.30 p.m. on channel 4. Over-the-edge comedy produced by New Yorkers trying to shock Angelenos, an impossibility.

4 Network news. In New York, CBS is on channel 2, NBC on 4, and ABC on 7. The 6 o'clock news shows on all three channels are a panoply of technical miracles: flipped images, remote broadcasting, wizard computer graphics. Brief and gossamer coverage of the news.

5 Channel 13. Public television, which seems to run mostly imports from Thames TV and the BBC, is the only possible choice for non-flashy video and any degree of depth. Big on nature and art. The MacNeil-Lehrer News Hour, nightly at 7.30 p.m., is leisurely, focussed and thoughtful.

6 Cable. Dominated by religion and sports. For terrifying fundamentalist rhetoric, see Jimmy Swaggart; for sheer ooze, and just as scary, Jerry Falwell and the Moral Majority. MTV (rock video) is a blissful antidote, well worth dipping into. Or you can catch up on American football, formerly confined to the autumn, now inescapable.

Radio: On FM radio (which corresponds to British VHF), the commercial classical stations are WNCN (104.3 MHz) and WQXR (96.3). WBAI (99.5) is independent and non-profit-making; no one even comes close for range of programming. WKCR (89.9 MHz) is great for jazz. The best news programmes are produced by National Public Radio on WNYC (94 MHz): 'Morning Edition', from 6.00 to 8.30 a.m., and 'All Things Considered', from 5.00 to 6.30 p.m. The rock stations on FM range from avant-garde to blah, and since they constantly seem to change formats there's no point in listing them here.

AM radio (i.e. medium wave) is about 75 per cent raucous and the rest soporific. Rock, easy listening (aka 'beautiful music'), country-and-western, and talk-back shows.

Newspapers: The *New York Times* is still one of the world's best papers. The *Sunday Times* weighs about a stone, and goes on sale at 8.30 p.m. on Saturday: if you want to keep your Sunday free, it's a good idea to spend all night dealing with it. The daily editions each include a special section: Science, 'Living' (i.e. food), the Home, 'Weekend' (entertainment). Best bets: Metropolitan Diary, which eavesdrops brilliantly on the city, and William Geist's 'About New York' column. Daily cost, 30¢; Sunday, $1.25.

The *New York Post*
A glance at the headlines will give you a clue. The *Post* is rapidly going the way of America's self-parody rag, the *National Enquirer* . . . stories of the order of 'Headless Body Found in Topless Bar'.

The *Daily News*
A battered contender for the *Post's* audience: a shade more attention to reality, and a few good columnists; for militant, irascible New Yorkism, Jimmy Breslin is the one to keep your eye on. Daily, 30¢

The *Village Voice*
An entrenched alternative, the *Voice* has been in a running battle with the city, state and federal governments since its inception. Most of the politics won't make sense to out-of-towners (or many in-towners, for that matter), but the reportage on art, music, film,

dance and popular culture is provocative and generally excellent. And it runs the city's best rock 'n' roll calendar. Weekly, $1.

Magazines:

The New Yorker
Impudent in 1925; now a grande dame. You wouldn't want to advertise anything less than a Silver Cloud in its pages. Watch for Calvin Trillin's matchless articles on American food; Roger Angell's baseball columns; V. S. Pritchett on books. In the front of the book are 'Goings on About Town', capsule reviews and calendars of plays, films, concerts, art shows, dance, night clubs: more discriminating than comprehensive. $1.50, weekly.

New York magazine
Deals with urban problems that affect the upwardly mobile: neighbourhood gentrification, restaurant trends, interior decoration, fashionable gossip. Invaluable for its all-inclusive calendars of events (including radio and TV), and for the weekly 'Sales and Bargains' column by Lenore Fleischer. The London *Times* crossword appears at the back, I suspect only to appease expatriate Britons. $1.75, weekly.

The New York Review of Books
The country's tweediest radical journal, most of it written from beyond the grave by Sartre. Political cartoons by David Levine make it worth at least a casual browse, and the personal ads at the back are classic.

Money

See Preliminaries, p.15, for an idea of how much to bring with you.

Denominations:

Notes (called bills) are standard in size and colour, and only US presidents (plus one Treasury Secretary and one kite flyer) get to have their pictures on them. $1 (Washington), $2 (Jefferson; something of a rarity; revived in the Nixon administration), $5 (Lincoln), $10 (Hamilton), $20 (Jackson), $50 (Grant), $100 (Franklin). There are some higher denominations but no one ever lays eyes on them. Cab drivers may baulk at 20-dollar bills, while restaurants will usually take twenties and fifties, especially if they get the lion's share.

US coinage runs from the 'silver' dollar (virtually extinct, although half-heartedly revived during the Carter administration. In an attempt at feminism, the Mint embossed a likeness of the suffragette Susan B. Anthony on it, resulting in extreme distress in the macho community . . .) to the half-dollar (fifty cents, and medium-rare, because it doesn't work in coin-op machines; Kennedy on the obverse), the quarter (twenty-five cents, Washington), the dime (ten cents, Roosevelt), the nickel (five cents – Jefferson on most, Crazy Horse still to be found on a few) and the penny (one cent, Lincoln).

Because virtually everything has 8¼ per cent city/state tax tacked on, you'll find yourself trying to get rid of pockets-full of pennies. Fortunately, they're quite small.

You'll get odd looks unless you use correct terminology for money: $1.50 is 'a dollar fifty' or 'one-fifty', not 'one dollar fifty'.

Foreign exchange

Deak-Perera

International Arrivals Building, JFK Airport

Bank of America

TWA Terminal, JFK Airport

For a quick fix at Kennedy, you can change pounds to dollars (or to 119 other currencies, for that matter) 365 days a year. The rates may not be ideal, but if you land on New Year's Day it will tide you over.

In the city, try (but call for rates in advance):

Bank Leumi

535 Seventh Avenue (between 39th and 40th Streets)
382–4410

Thomas Cook

18 East 48th Street
310–9400

Deak-Perera

41 East 42nd Street
883–0400

Money Shop

5 West 42nd Street
586–1487

Open Saturdays, 9.30 a.m.–3.30 p.m.

Nuisances

The number one nuisance in New York is noise, and there's no real escape from it. The garbage trucks grind away at all hours, the gridlocks provoke orgies of horn-blowing, and New Yorkers have a tradition of shouting their conversations across the street. The invention of the theft alarm for cars (which deters no one, and blasts off at the touch of a falling leaf) has ripped away the last shreds of quiet in the city. Your only relief will be an inside room in your hotel, with a view of the airshaft, and plenty of walks in Central Park, where the trees filter out the mayhem.

In the subways, the rattle of the express trains is ear-shattering, and if you want to preserve your hearing you should invest in ear plugs: the little foam ones worn by construction workers are available at hardware stores.

Other problems:

Beggars turn up in unlikely spots such as the Upper East Side, where charity is not even cold, but non-existent. The traditional territory for bottomed-out alcoholics is on the Bowery, in the Lower East Side, and it's to be avoided. The homeless – as a result of some ill-advised city housing manoeuvres, combined with a callous mass amnesty for the mentally ill – are omnipresent. Generally they do not beg, but subsist.

Rubbish ('garbage') in all its incarnations. New Yorkers blithely and unconsciously litter the streets and subways with newspapers, candy wrappers, paper cups, anything that passes through their hands. Nothing stops them: not laws, not even advertising. For major rubbish events, the best time to be in New York is during a sanitation workers' strike. The last one I witnessed was awesome.

Smoking in America is slowly being cordoned out of existence. It's prohibited in public transport and theatre auditoria, and in department stores and some supermarkets. Virtually every restaurant has a non-smoking section, and non-smokers are becoming increasingly vociferous about second-hand smoke. So watch it.

Police

The classic New York truism, on the subject of cops, is that they're never there when you need them. Not entirely accurate: the fact is that the city is crawling with cops, and they're all in cars. The cop on the beat – the foot patrol – is all but extinct but rumoured to be on the verge of a comeback. If you need about ten squad cars in a hurry, dial 911.

Post

Rates:

Domestic letter	$0.22 first half ounce;
	0.17 each additional ounce
postcard	0.14
Overseas letter	0.44 per half ounce, airmail
postcard	0.33
'mailgram'	0.36
Air parcel post to Britain	4.60 first 4 ounce
	0.90 each additional 4 ounces or fraction

Post boxes ('mail boxes') are rather small and painted blue, with a sort of upside-down trap-door mechanism for depositing letters.

Some of the more central post offices:

Ansonia Station, 1990 Broadway
Grand Central Station, 450 Lexington Avenue
Lenox Hill Station, 217 East 70th Street
Madison Square Station, 149 East 23rd Street

Murray Hill Station, 115 East 34th Street
Old Chelsea Station, 217 West 18th Street
Radio City Station, 322 West 52nd Street
Rockefeller Center Station, 610 Fifth Avenue

General Post Office

421 Eighth Avenue (between 31st and 33rd Streets)

This is the one with the Corinthian columns and the line from Herodotus incised in stone: 'Neither snow nor rain nor heat nor gloom of night stays these couriers from the swift completion of their appointed rounds.' It gives me a chill every time I see it. For a kind of end-of-the-world party atmosphere, the GPO steps are the place to be between 11.00 p.m. and midnight, 15 April, just before the annual income-tax deadline.

Safety

Malicious rumour to the contrary, New York does *not* have the highest crime rate in the country. It has a lot of crime, but it's got a big population. And the city also has by far the biggest police force in the country – twice the size of Chicago's (the next largest).

It's a waste of time to be paranoid about your safety in the city: just be prudent. Stay out of unpopulated places, especially at night, especially alone. Stay alert. Don't creep around – walk with your head up.

Women should keep a grip on handbags in the street, and hold them on their laps on subways, in restaurants, everywhere they sit. The breast pocket, rather than the hip, is the place for a man's wallet. If you have jewellery that you'd rather keep, either leave it at home or keep it tucked under your clothes when you're outdoors.

Subway robberies are increasingly common: in the trains late at night and in the more hectic stations (Times Square is notorious). Pickpockets and purse snatchers are always in the neighbourhood, and children between 9 and 17 years old are the most adept. They're looking for open handbags, wallet outlines, distracted attitudes. They're interested only in people who look like victims. Make sure that's not you.

If you do happen to get held up, it's said to be wise to hand over the goods without complaint: don't struggle unless your life is on the line. In situations of assault, there are several schools of thought – from passive to active resistance – and the most appropriate one is up to you.

Telephones

Even after the demonopolization of 'Ma Bell' a few years ago, the American phone system is still the best on earth: it works, and it's cheap. With the introduction of competitive long-distance companies, and the splitting of AT&T into regional corporations, the price of local calls has risen while long-distance rates (within the US) have gone down.

You'll find public telephones ('pay phones', in 'phone booths') on almost every corner of midtown Manhattan, and almost all of them work – despite the best efforts of the forces of vandalism. The phone company doesn't even attempt to leave directories in the booths, and you won't find one anywhere outside Grand Central Terminal, which has banks of them at the east end of the Grand Concourse. But a call to 'Directory Assistance' is free and the information is immediate. The Manhattan/Bronx information number is 411. More often than not a computer will read the number to you . . . twice, out of pity for mankind's short memory. All long-distance calls (including those to Brooklyn and Queens) are preceded by '1'.

If you should want to call Directory Assistance in Omaha, you'd dial

1	402	555–1212
[direct dial access]	[area code]	[universal D.A. number]

If you need operator assistance (e.g. for a 'collect' call,), replace the '1' with a zero and dial the remaining numbers.

Direct dial to London:

1	44	1
[access]	[country code]	[city code]
		XXX–XXXX
		[number]

A 10-minute call to London will cost you $7.60 at 'economy' rates

(6.00 p.m. to 7.00 a.m.), or $9.50 at 'discount' rates (1.00 p.m. to 6.00 p.m.), or $12.60 at 'standard' rates (7.00 a.m. to 1.00 p.m.).

Local calls from public phones now cost 25¢ including area code 718 calls to Brooklyn and Queens. Insert the coins before you start dialling. If you make calls – especially long-distance – from a hotel room, you can be quite sure that the rates will be substantially padded. The alternatives are to reverse the charges or carry a pocketful of quarters to the closest and quietest phone booth you can find.

The various sounds you'll hear:

1 a continuous hum = dial tone
2 repeated purring noise = ringing
3 repeated beep = engaged ('busy signal')
4 an infinite number of recorded messages, and Muzak when you're put on 'hold'.

Time

If you do plan to call home, remember that it's 5 hours *later* in Britain than in New York. If you place a call to London at 9.00 p.m., the party on the other end probably won't want to talk to you.

Tipping

In **restaurants:** New York's 8¼ per cent sales tax makes tipping easy even for people like me, who are showered with confusion at the end of every meal. Just double the tax and add it to the bill: a perfect 16.5 per cent. Add a little for good service; subtract for bad. If you insist on exact calculation, remember to tip only a percentage of the pre-tax portion of the bill, not the bottom line.

Some New York waiters, especially in the crustier venues, have a tendency to confuse unctuousness with good service. It's a habit you need not reward.

In **cabs:** Tip on the fare as it comes off the meter: a straight 20 per cent for a basic ride; more, or less, in exceptional circumstances.

Porters: $1 for up to three bags. In hotels, porters are called 'bell-hops'.

Traffic

For pure madness, New York traffic is a match for that of London, Paris or Rome (but notably more tranquil than Boston's). Anyone behind the wheel in New York is robbed of any residual sweetness of disposition. Bad tempers and congenital pushiness cause accidents (you'll hardly ever see an undented car in the city, much less a clean one), clogged streets, and gridlocks at intersections. Traffic lights and lanes are absolutely meaningless. Potholes the size of the Grand Canyon are rife. Taxis use anything that moves as a target, and trucks like to park for hours in the middle of the street, especially at rush hour. It's bad enough to be a pedestrian in conditions like these – to be a driver is positively unhealthy. If you insist on driving in New York, you'll need to get an International Driver's Licence before you arrive in the US. Before you get behind the wheel, stop by the Motor Vehicles Dept, 155 Worth Street, for a copy of the local rules of the road. A rabbit's foot hanging from the rear-view mirror helps, too. Remember: American traffic runs on the right-hand side of the road.

Wheelchair access

Most kerbs are now ramped at street corners (this makes life easier for roller skaters, too); museums and other public buildings have retrofitted their entrances; and New Yorkers travel everywhere by elevator – so it's perfectly possible to get around locally. Distance is another matter: you can forget about the subway and the bus. If you plan to travel by taxi, you can still occasionally find one of the big 'Checker' cabs, which are easy to get in and out of – but they're getting scarce. And it's pointless to try to hail a cab from a wheelchair: you'll need a friend or a decoy to do it for you.

For thorough coverage of the question, get a copy of *Access New York*, available free from the Junior League of New York, 130 East 80th Street, New York, NY 10021.

Emergencies

911 is the phone number to remember – for police, fire department, or ambulance.

Ambulance

Dial 911. Not a public service: it'll cost you a bundle. A recent 9-block tour of midtown Manhattan, with paramedics, cost $130. Another good reason to stock up on insurance.

Consulates

British Consulate General
845 Third Avenue
752–8400

Australian Consulate General
636 Fifth Avenue
245–4000

New Zealand Consulate General
630 Fifth Avenue
586–0060

Hot lines

Alcoholics Anonymous: 473–6200
Animal bites: 566–7105
Crime victims hotline: 577–7777 (24 hours)
Gay and lesbian health concerns: 566–6110
Noise complaints: 966–7500
Poison Control: 340–4494
Rape help line: 732–7706
Suicide prevention help line: 532–2400 (24 hours)
Traveler's Aid Services: 944–0013
VD clinic information: 226–5353

Lost credit cards

Somewhere in your luggage you've got a providential scrap of paper
with the numbers, expiration date and *New York addresses* of the
issuing companies. All you have to do is find each company in the
phone book and call in the numbers. They'll put a stop-payment
on your cards and with luck you won't even have to pay the
'maximum loss' fee. Now, if you can only find that scrap of paper.

Lost passport

If you don't know your passport number by heart, write it down
somewhere. Report a lost or stolen passport to the police (dial 911
if you've actually been held up; otherwise 374–5000), and then
head for your Consul General (p.204), who will fix you up with a
temporary document.

Lost traveller's cheques

You've been keeping track of the cheque numbers all along, dutifully
crossing them off whenever you pick up some cash . . . so it's no

problem to phone in the numbers of the missing cheques to the company that issued them. Nowadays, American Express is more or less staking its life on replacing TCs within hours, which means that the other big companies will be trying at least as hard.

Medical problems

Most American health care is emphatically private, and the cost is borne by high insurance rates. It's *vital* that you buy adequate health insurance before you leave home. See Preliminaries, p.16.

For non-emergencies, if you can't get find someone to recommend a physician, the private clinics are your best bet. The comprehensive list is in the Yellow Pages (under Clinics), and finding the right one will take some work: first you'll have to weed out the sex therapists, abortion centres, marriage counsellors and obesity consultants; then you'll have to make some phone calls. How long before you can get an appointment? What accreditation does the clinic have? How much will treatment cost? Will your insurance cover it? Do they take credit cards?

The following (city-run and private) are full-service hospitals, with emergency rooms.

Bellevue Hospital Center

First Avenue and 27th Street
561–4141

Beth Israel Medical Center

Stuyvesant Square (19th Street and Second Avenue)
420–2000

Lenox Hill Hospital

Park Avenue and 77th Street
794–4567

Mt Sinai Medical Center

Fifth Avenue at 100th Street
650–6500

St Vincent's Hospital

Seventh Avenue and 11th Street
790–7000

Pharmacies

A.k.a. drugstores. The following keep odd hours:

Bigelow Pharmacy

414 Sixth Avenue (between 8th and 9th Streets)
533–2700

Hours: Monday–Friday, 8.00 a.m.–9.00 p.m.
Saturday, 8.00 a.m.–7.00 p.m. Sundays/holidays,
9.00 a.m.–6.00 p.m. A courteous, old-fashioned institution which
only recently dismantled its soda-fountain – but uncovered a
beautiful mosaic floor in the process.

Boyd Chemists

655 Madison Avenue (at 60th Street)
838–6558

Hours: Monday–Friday, 9.30 a.m.–7.00 p.m.
Saturday, 9.30 a.m.–6.00 p.m.
Any drugstore that calls itself 'Chemists' will escalate its prices
shamelessly . . . but late hours may compensate somewhat.
Cards: AE, MC, V.

Kaufman Pharmacy

Lexington Avenue at 50th Street.
755–2266

Hours: 7 days, 24 hours
Cards: AE, MC, V.

La Rochelle Pharmacy

366 Amsterdam Avenue (at 78th Street)
877–4185

Hours: Monday–Friday, 10.00 a.m.–7.30 p.m.
Saturday, 10.00 a.m.–6.00 p.m.
Cards: AE only.

Martin's Drug Store

451 Third Avenue (at 31st Street)
685–5230

Hours: Monday-Friday, 9.00 a.m.–10.00 p.m.
Saturday, 9.00 a.m.–9.00 p.m. Sunday, 9.00 a.m.–6.00 p.m.
Cards: AE, MC, V.

Plaza Pharmacy

86th Street and Second Avenue
879–3878

Hours: Monday–Sunday, 10.00 a.m.–midnight. Cards: AE, MC, V.

Police

Dial 911 in an emergency.
For non-emergencies, call 374–5000 to find out your local precinct number.

Index

Non-fiction

☐ **The Money Book**	Margaret Allen	£4.95p
☐ **Fall of Fortresses**	Elmer Bendiner	£1.75p
☐ **The Love You Make**	Peter Brown and	
	Steven Gaines	£2.95p
☐ **100 Great British Weekends**	John Carter	£2.95p
☐ **Last Waltz in Vienna**	George Clare	£1.95p
☐ **Walker's Britain**	Andrew Duncan	£5.95p
☐ **Travellers' Britain**	Arthur Eperon	£2.95p
☐ **The Tropical Traveller**	John Hatt	£2.95p
☐ **The Lord God Made Them All**	James Herriot	£2.50p
☐ **The Neck of the Giraffe**	Francis Hitching	£2.50p
☐ **A Small Town is a World**	David Kossoff	£1.00p
☐ **Prayers and Graces**	Allen Laing	
	illus. by Mervyn Peake	£1.25p
☐ **Best of Shrdlu**	Denys Parsons	£1.50p
☐ **The New Small Garden**	C. E. Lucas Phillips	£2.50p
☐ **Thy Neighbour's Wife**	Gay Talese	£2.50p
☐ **Dead Funny**	Fritz Spiegl	£1.50p
☐ **Future Shock**	Alvin Toffler	£2.95p
☐ **The World Atlas of Treasure**	Derek Wilson	£6.50p

All these books are available at your local bookshop or newsagent, or
can be ordered direct from the publisher. Indicate the number of copies
required and fill in the form below   12
....

Name_____
(Block letters please)

Address_____

_____

Send to CS Department, Pan Books Ltd, PO Box 40, Basingstoke, Hants
Please enclose remittance to the value of the cover price plus:
35p for the first book plus 15p per copy for each additional book ordered
to a maximum charge of £1.25 to cover postage and packing
Applicable only in the UK

While every effort is made to keep prices low, it is sometimes
necessary to increase prices at short notice. Pan Books reserve
the right to show on covers and charge new retail prices which
may differ from those advertised in the text or elsewhere